RAISING CAIN

- How do birth order and age difference affect children?
- Do parents' own sibling relationships influence those of their children?
- Can parents love all their children equally?
- How can siblings learn to help each other to get along?
- When is the best time to have another child?

The answers to these and many other questions are only pages away!

HERBERT S. STREAN, D.S.W., received his doctorate in social work from Columbia University and has taught at the Rutgers University Graduate School of Social Work for two decades. A trained psychoanalyst specializing in the treatment of children and adolescents, Dr. Strean is director of the New York Center for Psychoanalytic Training.

LUCY FREEMAN has published many popular books on psychology, including the bestselling *Fight Against Fears*. Her earlier books with Dr. Strean are *Freud and Women* and *Guilt: Letting Go*.

Raising Cain

How to Help Your Children Achieve a Happy Sibling Relationship

Herbert S. Strean D.S.W.
and Lucy Freeman

ST. MARTIN'S PRESS/NEW YORK

RAISING CAIN: HOW TO HELP YOUR CHILDREN ACHIEVE A HAPPY SIBLING RELATIONSHIP

Copyright © 1988 by Herbert S. Strean, D.S.W. and Lucy Freeman

All rights reserved. No part of this book may be used or reproduced in any manner whatsoever without written permission except in the case of brief quotations embodied in critical articles or reviews. For information address Facts on File Inc., 460 Park Avenue South, New York, N.Y. 10016.

Library of Congress Catalog Card Number: 87-8921

ISBN: 0-312-91601-9 Can. ISBN: 0-312-91602-7

Printed in the United States of America

Facts on File hardcover edition published 1988
First St. Martin's Press mass market edition/August 1989

10 9 8 7 6 5 4 3 2 1

CONTENTS

ACKNOWLEDGMENTS

We wish to thank, first of all, Gerard Helferich, executive editor of *Facts On File*, for his constructive help in planning and bringing this book to realization and for suggesting the title. We also wish to thank Ruth Wreschner, our literary agent, for suggesting the idea of this kind of book on siblings.

Our thanks go also to Marcia Strean, wife of Dr. Herbert Strean, for reading the manuscript and giving valuable suggestions, and Billy and Richard Strean, for adding to their father's understanding of sibling rivalry.

We wish to thank, too, Dr. Strean's patients who, though anonymous, provided examples of some of the difficulties siblings face. And last but not least, we wish to thank each other for sensitizing us to our own sibling problems and helping us become more loving siblings.

Herbert S. Strean
Lucy Freeman

PREFACE

Parents play an important part in the sibling relationship. Parents write much of the sibling script without being aware of it, and how parents handle the emotional outbursts, the stubbornness, or the complaints of siblings depends in part on the parents' own attitudes and feelings. This book will help parents to understand the complex sibling bond and will suggest practical solutions to common problems parents face in raising siblings. Our examples are taken from everyday life. As parents read this book they will be reminded of their own children, the children next door, and themselves as young siblings.

Occasionally, we will use examples from therapeutic work with children and their parents. It has been said that children and parents who need therapy are the same as those not in therapy—except more so. That is, all children have problems with sibling rivalry—the child in therapy may merely experience them more deeply. Similarly, all parents have their doubts and insecurities, angers, and ambivalences. Like so many things in life, it is merely a matter of degree.

Herbert S. Strean
Lucy Freeman

Raising Cain

1

T HE SIBLING'S DILEMMA

FRIEND OR ENEMY?

There is probably no more intense relationship than the sibling bond, except the bond between child and parent. Powerful feelings of both love and hate alternate, often swiftly, and brothers and sisters have to learn in their earliest years to control these intense feelings; to learn, in other words, what it took thousands of years for primitive man to learn—how to be civilized.

Torn by humankind's strongest emotions, not yet in full control of their feelings, siblings may help or hinder each other during the sometimes painful process of growing up. The full range of raw human emotions explode on the sibling scene, especially in the early years. The home is the setting in which both the most ardent ties of love are formed and the deepest hatreds simmer. The sibling slowly learns to accept both violent and loving desires, and becomes what adults call "socialized." Siblings may either help each other to accept the inherent difficulties of life or destroy each other's capacity to adjust to the demands of parents and society.

Not coincidentally, the first recorded sibling relationship, in the Bible, was one of rivalry and horror. Abel was murdered when Cain's jealousy overpowered him. This first rivalrous relationship has been reenacted in varying degrees, from controlled envy to uncontrollable fury often resulting in tragedy. But the sibling relationship is not only one of rivalry and revenge. There is also affection, friendship, dependency, protectiveness, generosity, and alliance against the parents. The sibling relationship contributes to the personality development of each sibling. The experiences between siblings can be enriching or constrictive, self-enhancing or self-destructive as the sibling travels through what Freud called "the human condition." Think of our many years of deep attachment to parents and siblings. We spend almost a quarter of our lives in the home where we grow up. No wonder the past remains so much a part of us, even when it lies buried in our unconscious, seemingly forgotten and often denied.

Because the sibling bond is so common, and so important, it is puzzling why both scientific and popular books about siblings have been so scarce. Many vital questions remain unanswered. How can the rivalry and envy of siblings be eased so siblings—and parents—may enjoy more family peace? How does the parents' relationship affect the siblings'? Is the only child happier than a child with siblings? How does the age of a child affect how he is influenced by his siblings? These are just a few of the questions we will raise over the course of this book.

No one wishes to be torn by such contradictory emotions as love and hate so much of the time. It is easier for both children and adults to deny their hate and jealousy. To understand the sibling relationship is to accept that we all possess contradictory feelings of love and hatred. It is a matter of the love being stronger than the hate so we can get along with others and, even more importantly, feel self-esteem. For hatred carries with it the shadow of guilt, which saps our confidence in ourselves.

Sibling hatred stems from the natural feelings in all children after the birth of a sibling as they lose the coveted position of the little prince or princess of the household. Adjusting to the newcomer serves as a small but important arena for learning to get along as adults in the real world. We all want to be special. As children, when we feel hungry we are fed, when we are upset or uncomfortable we are soothed, when we are sick we are given medicine and extra care. It is frustrating to grow up and to realize that life is not all milk and honey. To accept that we can never be king or queen for more than a day is not easy. Who enjoys being supplanted by a rival?

THE LIMITS OF SIBLING RIVALRY

Sometimes, sibling hatred can lead to ostracism. Sometimes it is short-lived. But it always exists to some degree. To deny the hatred is to give up the chance of easing it and of allowing love to prevail. What we face we can conquer.

Selma Fraiberg in *The Magic Years* talks of "the right to sibling rivalry." She encourages parents to protect those rights. But, she points out, the right to feel anger and resentment is not a license to inflict it on others. A child may have "the right to feel angry and to give expression to his feelings—within certain limits," but a child should not be permitted to strike younger children or his parents, or to use abusive language as verbal aggression. Fraiberg counsels, "A child can be permitted to express his anger without resorting to savage name-calling. If he does so, if he loses control, he needs to know from his parents that he has overstepped the line."

Physical attacks by siblings on each other are regarded by many parents as a natural accompaniment to family life. Fraiberg comments, "'Just as long as they don't murder each other,' parents may say indulgently. Yet I can think of no good reason why children beyond the nursery age should settle their differences through jungle tactics, and even in the nursery years we should begin the education away from physical attack."

She describes households where nine- and ten-year-old boys and girls continue a war that began the day a baby came home from the hospital. The quarrels of the older children were like the quarrels of toddlers. "She's sitting in my chair!" or, "He got a bigger piece of pie than I did!" The result: "Tears. Stamping of feet. A slap. Shrieks. A deadly battle is on."

Fraiberg suggests such behavior occurs because the older children are not required to give up "infantile forms of rivalry." Parents fail to intervene and prevent their children from attacking each other through verbal or subtler forms of aggression. As Fraiberg puts it, "In the name of sibling rivalry, children today are permitted extraordinary license in cruel name-calling and refined torments designed to undermine each other's personalities."

She cites the case of an older sister who made a career of depreciating the masculinity of a younger brother. She undermined his self-confidence with taunts, disparaging remarks, and cruel jokes. Her parents shrugged their shoulders, saying: "Brothers and sisters will fight, you know." They did not try to stop their daughter and help her overcome her envy and aggressive feelings toward her brother; instead they allowed her to continue to damage the development of his character.

THE UNDERLYING DILEMMA

The sibling relationship is a dilemma of conflicting feelings, a web of love merged with hate. One day the sibling is capable of great self-sacrifice for a brother or sister, while the next day he may unleash a verbal or physical attack on a sibling who has irritated or criticized him or of whom he is envious.

A fifteen-year-old boy praised his seventeen-year-old brother for his prowess on the basketball team. A few hours later, learning that his brother had been accepted by an Ivy League college, the younger sibling berated his older brother angrily, calling him arrogant and selfish, for no apparent reason. He obviously was jealous of his brother's academic success.

Similarly, a six-year-old girl, Melinda, describing her two-year-old sister, said, "She's cute and pretty," then added thoughtfully, "But Mommy and Daddy love her better than me and I want to get rid of her." A few days later she grabbed a knife and walked menacingly toward her little sister. Fortunately, her parents stopped her in time from inflicting any wound.

Melinda loved her sister but hated her too. This universal sibling conflict is difficult for a child to face and resolve. Every child has to live with intense feelings of love and hate for each person in the famiy. As a ten-year-old girl said to a friend about her eight-year-old brother, "He's my darling when he's nice to me, but I hate him when he hits me."

Parents can reduce sibling hatred by starting with the premise that anger is inevitable and that siblings have a right to feel anger. Paradoxically, parents who want to curb sibling rivalry and hatred must first accept that children have a right to feel it.

When Melinda's parents helped her accept and face her anger, her murderous feelings gradually diminished. Often, when parents observe a child acting provocatively and cruelly toward a sibling, the angry child is asking for limits, for controls, for structure. Frequently, a fist-fight between siblings, or hostile name-calling, is a disguised cry for help. Parents who observe their children fighting would do well to convey two feelings to the children: that the parents understand the anger and resentment and accept it as normal, and that, nevertheless, the parents cannot allow one child to hurt another with acts or words.

THERE'S NO SUCH THING AS EXCLUSIVE LOVE

Sometime in the early years siblings have to accept the impossibility of obtaining the exclusive love of a parent. A parent may feel more love for one child than for another, but there is usually some degree of love bestowed on each sibling. As siblings realize and accept this, their hostility eases and they are able to acknowledge that each of them will be loved for his or her own qualities and achievements. They do not need to live in constant anger, feeling unloved.

One father told his twelve-year-old daughter, who was envious of her ten-year-old brother, "I don't expect you to be perfect. I get angry at times too. But I do expect you to share my love, and your mother's love, with your brother. You cannot demand exclusive right to it. We are a family. We should be able to live together in harmony, helping each other, not tearing each other down."

He was telling his daughter that he loved her, but that he also loved her brother and that she should not expect all his love. He was also asking her to give up some of her self-love. He was saying, in essence, that love has to be learned, and that she had to learn to relinquish some of her selfishness and become a cooperative member of the family.

There may be initial jealousy and rivalry when the older child finds himself displaced by younger siblings, but when his hostile feelings turn into friendly ones in the interest of getting along with the other family members, the jealous hatreds are forgotten.

One of the important issues in the sibling relationship is learning to share. They share parents. They share possessions, sometimes even clothes. They may share the same bedroom, the same closet, the same bathroom. It is difficult to give up the childhood wish to "have it all." Sharing stirs emotions of envy, competition, and hostility—feelings that are difficult to acknowledge and painful to accept.

But, siblings do learn to share, to their later advantage. In fact, if they go away to college they feel lonely, yearning for their brothers or sisters. College sororities and fraternities would not exist if the lonely student did not seek a replacement for the lost sibling. (The members even refer to themselves as "brothers" and "sisters.") Some colleges and universities that prohibit fraternities and sororities provide what is called the "house plan," where students find a home away from home, complete with "siblings."

However, the activities of fraternities and sororities also show siblings' mixed emotions. Though the members are nominally brothers or sisters who pledge to support each other, they will, at times, hurt each other, even commit sadistic pranks, sometimes even accidentally maim or kill a member in initiation rites. Fraternities and sororities reflect in microcosm what goes on among real brothers and sisters: an intense love and loyalty, but also hatred and the desire to hurt.

THE PARENTS' EXAMPLES

It is a truism that all children are extremely vulnerable, their feelings are easily hurt. The psychic wounds of the earliest years are the ones that cause emotional damage. At the same time there can be a happy medium in solving the inevitable conflicts of sibling rivalry. Each child must be helped to respect the other, to refrain from attacks on self-esteem. In a family where respect for all the members is low, there will be little harmony between siblings.

Giving up the pleasures of infancy, which are selfish pleasures for the most part, is not easy. But when parents show in their own relationship that cooperation is enjoyable and brings the reward of friendship, siblings learn to love each other more than they hate each other.

Siblings can have an enjoyable, easy, relationship which lays the foundation for future relationships outside the home. But, they need their parents to show the way. Siblings, no matter what their age, are helpless when it comes to giving up the fantasy that they are perfect and that all their demands should be met. Parents must show that adjusting to society's demands will bring the greatest reward—love.

To help siblings share, parents need to be convinced that sharing is commendable. How much parents share with each other serves as a model for their children. If parents compete rather than share, their children will compete rather than share. One of the reasons both adults and children become hesitant about sharing is that they believe sharing means giving up something. They feel that if they share, they will have less pleasure. If they share toys, they will have fewer possessions. If they share parents, they will have less love. Parents need to emphasize that sharing makes life fuller and happier. If a brother shares a toy with his sister, the pleasure of both increase. There is joy in sharing, self-hatred in selfishness. No one likes a selfish person. The giver is always welcome.

In the next chapter, we will explore further the idea that parents in large part, set the tone for the siblings' relationships.

A minister sought help when his eighteen-year-old son was caught stealing a car. The minister was very upset as he described how his son was taken to the police station after driving a neighbor's car out of the yard. The neighbor had chased him in another car and caught him. But the therapist noticed how excited the minister became as he described the chase with a gleam of pleasure in his eyes.

"Part of you seems to have gotten a kick out of what your son did," the therapist remarked.

At first, the minister strongly denied this. But, a few sessions later he told the therapist he now agreed that he had vicariously enjoyed his son's crime and had wanted him to get away with it rather than be caught and punished. The minister said with a half-smile, "I guess the pious, law-abiding side of me occasionally would like to be defeated by a more wanton part."

"We all feel that way," the therapist reassured him. "We learn to repress our primitive wishes, like the wish to steal what we covet. But the wishes always exist and at times may conquer our wish to obey the law."

The therapist helped the minister understand that his son had sensed these wishes to rebel and had carried them into action. An understanding judge granted the son probation on condition he receive therapy, a decision the boy's father heartily endorsed.

THE INFLUENCE OF THE PARENT'S SIBLINGS

A physical education teacher was worried about his son. The father was upset because his son was a poor athlete and shy with his peers. He realized he was embarrassed to acknowledge that he, an athletic, virile man who had many friends, was rearing a son who was emerging as the antithesis of all his ideals. The father recalled his brother, two years older, whom he had always envied and resented. This brother had become a well-known lawyer for a large movie corporation in Los Angeles and lived in a lavish home in Beverly Hills. The brother had surpassed him when they were in high school on the baseball field, in the classroom, and evidently in all else. As he faced his feelings of envy, competition, and resentment toward his brother, he became aware that what he was doing to his son was what he had wished to do to his brother—demean him, cut him down, and kill his competitive spirit.

Parents sometimes treat a child like a rival of both the present (taking the mother's love away from the father, or the father's love away from the mother) and of the past (one of the parent's own siblings who took away a mother's or father's love). This father had been unconsciously trying to emotionally demolish his son as he had wished, as a boy, to demolish his successful older brother. Consciously, he wanted his son to be the winner he himself never was. But a stronger desire—to destroy his enemy of years past who, he believed, had kept him from being a winner—caused him to treat his son with contempt. Contempt may be more painful to a child than a slap across the face. Many sons of athletes turn out to be nonathletes. The father has converted his son into an opponent of the past, usually a rivalrous sibling, but a rival he can now defeat. In fantasy the father has become the sibling he envied, no longer his inferior self. He has used his son to turn childhood defeat into adult victory. The powerful wishes, hurts, and envies of the past can seek resolution and revenge in the present if we are not aware of our hidden fantasies and the intense emotions still struggling within.

The more successfully parents can face their hidden resentments, the less resentful a child they will have. One of the reasons it is difficult for parents to accept their own resentments is that they judge themselves too harshly. Just as sibling rivalry is a universal phenomenon, parental resentment also is, and should not be harshly condemned. When parents accept their resentments from both the past and present and share them with their spouses, the less judgmental they will be and less resentment will appear in their children.

A mother brought Alice, her six-year-old daughter, for therapy. Alice had suddenly started to regress, after the birth of a sister. Alice demanded that she be diapered, sucked her thumb, wet her bed, and indulged in baby talk. Such regression is not unusual at the birth of a sibling, as the older child tries to compete with the seemingly favored arrival.

The mother told the therapist that she had a younger sister to whom she did not speak and had always disliked. She also described how she felt when her sister was born and how she, like Alice, had started sucking her thumb again, wetting her pants, and speaking baby talk. The hate she felt toward her younger sister was communicated unconsciously to her older daughter. The mother had accepted, as inevitable, mutual hatred between the siblings. Such powerful feelings from the past can be like blueprints for building present emotional structures.

A thirty-five-year-old mother confessed to her therapist that she felt distant and remote from her twelve-year-old son. "He's a handsome boy and very bright," she said. "But I feel as though I must hold back all signs of love. What's the matter with me? I hate myself for not being more affectionate."

She remembered that as a girl she was "madly in love" with her older, very handsome, charming brother. She confessed she had sexual fantasies about him while growing up. She had transferred this guilty love for her brother to her equally handsome son and then, to protect herself from these uncomfortable feelings, kept a discreet physical distance from him. This is another way parents transfer the feelings about their siblings onto their children.

Many fathers hold back warm feelings toward their daughters because they unconsciously view them as the sisters whom they wanted to hug, kiss, and love sexually. They fantasize that if they kiss their daughters, even innocently, they are kissing their verboten sisters.

A little girl of eight was heartbroken when her father suddenly stopped allowing her to sit on his lap and withdrew from her when she wanted to hug and kiss him. He said sternly, "You're too old for that nonsense." He felt guilty because he was transferring to her the sensual feelings he had felt, as a boy, for his beautiful older sister. He had even named his daughter after this sister, and he now transferred the love to his daughter.

Often parents, when they face the fact that they have fantasized their child as a sibling, feel more comfortable in bestowing physical affection. When parents were children, if they did not have physically demonstrative parents, they are also likely to behave the same way with their own children. Sometimes, an inhibition toward physical affection on the part of parents can come from two factors: making the child act out a past sibling fantasy, or treating the child as the mother's or father's parents treated them. One of the best ways for parents to feel more comfortable sharing spontaneous intimacy with their children is for them to separate their past from their present, and to tell themselves that they can do better than their parents, as well as reassure themselves that their children are not their siblings.

When parents overindulge a child and fail to set limits, this behavior may often be traced to their sibling relationships. A young mother of twenty-nine could never say no to her nine-year-old daughter; she felt she was turning her daughter "into a spoiled brat," she told a friend. She explained, "I feel so helpless with her. I can't discipline her. I give her everything she wants and more."

Then this mother realized that, as she had grown up, she felt shortchanged and ignored by her parents. Her older brother was always the center of attention, given expensive toys, the highest-priced cars, and an education at an Ivy League college. She felt relegated to the back seat, the recipient of little attention, love, or generosity from her parents.

To compensate for her intense, long-stored-up feelings of deprivation and to express rage at her parents, the mother indulged her daughter in the way she wished she had been indulged. Though she knew she harmed her daughter by such wholesale indulgence, she could not stop it; and so she decided to seek help from a therapist.

Often an adult who asks for help ostensibly for a child is actually asking to be helped. The parent knows he or she is sabotaging the child's happiness by behavior he cannot control. When we fail to control acts we know are destructive to others or ourselves, we may need help to understand why we keep repeating such actions. This applies to all excessive behavior, from overeating to overwork. In sum, every excess carries within it the roots of its own destruction.

This mother, with the help of the therapist, tempered her

past resentments toward her brother and accepted the reality that he was not quite the little god she thought he was, nor was she quite the slave she believed she had been. She could then say quiet, appropriate no's to her daughter. The older a child is before learning to accept frustration, the more difficult it is to accept them. The child should learn the lesson early and gently that there are many times when our wishes cannot be gratified. Otherwise, the result may be a depressed, inwardly raging adult.

THE SIBLINGS' OWN CONTRIBUTIONS

A child is not merely a mirror of the parents, responding like a robot to the parents' signals, suggestions, and dreams. Each child interprets, embellishes, and distorts what he or she observes in the parents, hears from them, or imagines them to be. Every child is different in the vast memories and feelings carried since the cradle.

All of us share certain universal characteristics—the start of sexual desires at age three or four, a burst of rage when someone injures our self-esteem, the urge to eat so we will not die. But each of us stands alone when it comes to how we view what happened in our lives—our actual experiences and the fantasies about them are usually woven around love and hate and fashion our personalities.

The differences are shown in the various attitudes siblings have toward their parents. Some children will listen to a parent with far more interest than others. Some will idolize their parents more. Some seem intent on antagonizing their parents, others on pleasing them. The attitude depends on each child's memories of the parents' behavior toward him or her. Children's fantasies also play a vital part in viewing parents. For instance, all young children believe that they are omnipotent and that parents are gods who will grant every request. As children develop the ability to use reason they can eventually discern between these fantasies and the frustrations of reality, which makes a number of painful demands.

UNDERSTANDING WHY
SIBLINGS FIGHT

Some parents have difficulty breaking up fights between siblings because they feel helpless in coping with the many battles siblings invariably wage. When siblings fight, they are usually seeking to be the most loved child. When a five-year-old grabs a new toy that a three-year-old sibling has been given by their mother, the five-year-old is saying, "She loves me more, I came first, and this toy is mine." When a parent does not stop siblings from fighting, the parent, on some level, may want the fight to continue; part of the parent may enjoy the fight because the two competitors are fighting for parental love. Who does not wish to be fought over as the coveted object of love?

There is another reason for parental helplessness in the face of sibling combat. Often, when siblings engage in a fracas, a mother or father identifies with one child against the other, hoping for the preferred child's victory. The parent may even have unconsciously provoked the fight so that the child with whom the parent identifies would win.

A young mother who was unable to curb the fistfights between her two sons sought the help of a therapist. It became clear that she identified with the younger son and secretly wanted him to beat up his older brother. She told the therapist that she had grown up with an older brother whom she resented and wanted to vanquish but never could. Her wish that her younger son who, in her fantasy represented herself as a little girl, would be victorious kept her from stopping the fights. She silently cheered him on, hoping, as occasionally happened, that he would win. She would then feel a triumphant, long-awaited childhood victory.

In looking at marital partners, we often see that they are primarily sibling rivals rather than husband and wife. They fight to be the one and only, leaving their children with the impression that cooperation and sharing are not desirable, that winning the battle is what counts. The spirit of compromise, of accepting frustration and occasional defeat, is learned slowly even from wise parents.

We have pointed out that when sibling fighting continues, it is often because the parents gain vicarious pleasure from it. We have further suggested that parents may be either continuing their own earlier fights with siblings or are keeping alive fights with their own parents. The most difficult thing in the world for many adults is to give up their old family battles. We all seek revenge for ancient hurts, and it is understandable why so many of us want to keep the old fights going. But what frequently motivates parents to give up the fights of childhood is the recognition that when they do, the family life of their children improves.

For parents to love a child, the parents have to possess a certain amount of love and esteem for themselves. Not narcissistic love but mature love. Many of us do not love ourselves enough; therefore many parents find it difficult to love their children consistently. If a mother's or father's self-esteem is low, it is difficult, if not impossible, for her or him to hold the children in high esteem.

Parents may find it difficult to admit a lack of self-esteem or to accept the idea that they do not love their children enough—a love that holds trust and respect for the growing independence of the child. One little boy stormed at his possessive mother, "You gave me life but you don't own me!" Parents are often blind to the many difficulties inherent in raising children. For example, the parent may have been emotionally deprived as a child and may have difficulty comprehending the complexities involved in bringing up a fairly happy, adjusted youngster.

Freud said that there were three impossible professions: statesman, psychoanalyst, and parent. Parenthood is one of the most difficult tasks in the world. Almost anyone can produce a baby, but the years that follow demand a great deal of self-awareness on the part of the mother and father if they want their children to have a chance at achieving comfortable, pleasurable lives.

No mother or father can be that mythical "perfect" parent. All of us have to struggle with fears and angers from our earliest days. Many power struggles between parents and children over feeding problems, over toilet training, over the no's handed down by the parents as they try to socialize the children, still go on between parents and children as parents carry with

them the anger they endured as children, at the hands of both
their parents and their siblings.

OTHER CLUES TO THE
PARENTAL SCRIPT

There are many other factors that influence how a parent
interacts with a child. Among them is the position of the child
in the family. If a parent was a first-born, there is a tendency to
identify with the first-born and project on this child many of
the parent's own aspirations and wishes to achieve.

If a father is the first-born and a mother a younger sibling,
conflicts may occur in the child because each parent views the
child differently. A seven-year-old boy was failing in his
schoolwork. He was a first-born, like his father, who viewed
him as a great achiever. But his mother viewed him as she had
viewed her older brother—with envy and anger, jealous of his
being her parents' favorite. The boy sensed that to please his
mother, he must not be the achiever his father was pushing
him to be.

Thus, parents do not always view their children objectively
but see them through the lens of their own childhood images.
Therapists who work with children and parents ask the parents, "Who does this child represent to you? Is the child an
idealized part of you? An envied sister? A beloved brother? A
hated rival of your early years?"

There are always clues as to why a child is treated in a special way. A child may be given the name of one parent's mother or father and then becomes, in some part of the parent's
mind, like the namesake who was idealized but also feared. Or
the youngster may bear the name of a parent's sibling to whom
he felt close.

One father, a successful lawyer, named his son after his rival
younger brother, whom he was always "beating out" in sports,
studies, and then professionally. The father reflected his sibling rivalry with his son who, because of the age difference,
was easily beaten when he played golf or poker with his father.
The son was never much of a success and failed his law school

examinations, unable to accept himself as surpassing a father who needed to win every battle. The father was still fighting his sibling war in his fantasies.

A mother named her first child Anne, after her own mother, who had died when she was two. Her daughter became "saint" Anne, the "mother" who would save her and relieve all her suffering. This was a burden no child could bear, and the daughter failed to ease her mother's lifelong depression. Instead, the daughter sacrificed her own happiness because of her guilt at failing to provide her mother with all she lacked. The daughter never married and lived with her mother until the latter's death at eighty-two.

Another reason siblings tend to become alienated and angry at each other, rather than sharing and loving, is because parents view them in such different ways. One sibling is considered brilliant, another slow. One sibling may be treated with excessive kindness, another with violence or cruelty, or ignored. The siblings will then feel uncomfortable with each other, as the favored one feels guilty and the denigrated one feels envy, hatred, and guilt. Hatred is always accompanied by the shadow of guilt.

When parents want to enhance their relationship with their children and diminish the conflicts between the children, one exercise that is helpful is to ask: What do I like about myself and what do I dislike about myself? Therapists have found that the things parents dislike about themselves they tend to project unconsciously onto their children, and then they worry that their children mirror what they cannot bear in themselves.

For example, if a father worries about his own sense of masculinity, he may project this feeling on his son and then criticize his son as not manly enough. If a mother feels afraid of her right to assert herself, she may project this feeling on her quiet, submissive daughter and criticize her.

Parents help their children best when they acknowledge and try to understand their own limitations, instead of condemning themselves. A father who does not feel sufficiently masculine might ask himself, What is so dangerous about not being masculine? Why does it frighten me? instead of criticizing himself or his son. Similarly a mother might ask why she is condemning herself and her daughter for being too passive.

CAN PARENTS LOVE ALL
THEIR CHILDREN EQUALLY?

For siblings to love each other, they have to feel that they are loved equally by their parents. Otherwise, there is deep resentment on the part of the one who feels less loved, and gloating on the part of the favored one. Siblings then feel ill at ease with each other and quarrels are apt to erupt at the slightest provocation. But can a parent love all his children truly equally? Is this not asking the impossible?

We believe it is natural for a parent to favor one child over another, at least at certain times. In some cases the favoritism may last a lifetime. Usually, when favoritism exists, it emerges during certain periods of one child's development, such as late infancy or adolescence. Both parents may show the same kind or different kinds of favoritism.

Parents are entitled to their preferences. Yet most parents deny they have preferences, believing they are bad parents if they prefer one child over another. To have a preference is to be human, and it is the rare person who deals with two or more people who does not prefer one over the others, at least on occasion. Yet, when it comes to siblings, parents forget this universal phenomenon.

In the movie *Cool Hand Luke*, starring Paul Newman, Luke's mother tries to explain why she loves him better than she does his brother. "Sometimes you get a feeling about a child and sometimes you don't," she says. The reasons for her "feeling" only she could know. Perhaps she wanted Luke more than she did his brother, or she loved him because he was a happier, brighter child. Or resembled a husband she loved.

It is a fact of life that some children are born more loving, more attractive, more sensitive than others. Some are more prone to colic, some have a smiling response to life, some are whinier, some more muscular. Dr. Peter Neubauer, Anna Marie Weil and Dr. Augusta Alpert, authorities in child behavior, report that children have different "drive endowments," in that some are more energetic than others. If one baby sleeps well through the night, while another cries and whines, keeping the parents from much-needed sleep, the parents will probably feel less love for the latter baby.

circums tus

Similarly, some children are born under adverse circumstances. The parents may be ambivalent about having another baby. Or a child may come into the world when a parent is ill, or unemployed, or when a marriage is breaking apart. These are all factors in the way a parent responds to a child.

Parents should talk to each other about their preferences. If they honestly acknowledge their preferences and understand the reasons why they favor one child over another, they are usually able to modulate overt favoritism of one child. This helps siblings feel more emotionally secure. Parents have a responsibility to both themselves and their children to understand and try to tame their predilections. But they should not deny that their preferences exist.

We know that favoritism does not help any child. The preferred become spoiled and egotistical, the less preferred become insecure and feel inferior. The less partiality a parent is able to show toward one sibling, the better off all siblings will be. Even if parents do not overtly show their preferences, the children can sense them.

A father who could acknowledge he enjoyed playing catch with his ten-year-old son more than skipping rope with his eight-year-old daughter respected himself more when he could admit his preference to himself and to his wife. When she did not censor him but pointed out that this feeling was understandable, he paradoxically felt freer to skip rope with his daughter. When we directly face our conflicting feelings, we find we use less energy to deny the "bad" feeling and we tend to like ourselves better for our honesty. Parents always become better role models for their children when they are honest about their own emotions.

A mother finally admitted to herself that she preferred to shop with her teenage daughter rather than watch her teenage son play soccer. As a result of her awareness, she found herself less bored at her son's soccer games. She learned more about how soccer was played and identified more with her son as he made his moves on the field to help his team win. Had she not admitted her preferences to herself, she would have used her energy to deny them and would not have been able to feel any pleasure in the son's activity.

THE BATTLE FOR INDEPENDENCE

Just as siblings learn how to handle aggressive feelings from parents, they also learn how to become independent. The great war of everyone's childhood is the battle to break free emotionally from his or her parents. We never break completely free, for the wish to remain dependent is a very powerful one. But we need to break free to a large degree, in order to assure ourselves a sense of identity and to feel in control of our own life. As siblings grow, they copy the dependency patterns of their parents. If the mother is the strong, dominating parent who makes the major family decisions, while the father is passive and subordinate, often a brother and sister will emulate the pattern.

The late Dr. Margaret Mahler, internationally known psychoanalyst and a member of the New York Psychoanalytic Institute, did pioneering work on the need for children to separate emotionally from their mothers. Her research with mothers and children shows that a child should start to separate emotionally from the mother at about eighteen months. This is the first step toward what Mahler calls "individuation."

If parents have not been able to successfully separate emotionally from their own parents, they cannot permit their children to separate emotionally from them. This is part of the "tone" of emotional life that is handed down over the generations, as noted by Monica McGoldrick of Rutgers University, who theorizes that many emotional themes in a family, such as dependency and violence, are transmitted from one generation to the next.

A mother in her late thirties was still very emotionally attached to her mother. Even after her mother died, this woman asked herself, "What would mother do?" or, "What would mother think?" before she made a decision. She was so dominated by the image of her mother that she had little confidence in her own opinions. She could not allow her children to form a relationship except with her. She checked constantly to find out whom they saw and what they talked about when they were with friends or relatives. She experienced her children's attempt to establish lives of their own as a hostile act toward her. Her mother had made her feel that to develop a sense of her own identity would bring disapproval and perhaps abandonment by her mother.

Parents sometimes have great difficulty watching their children break free. One mother and father shed tears as they saw their first child, a boy, stand up and walk on his own, as though he was preparing to leave them forever, no longer a pliant, helpless baby dependent on them. Another mother and father became depressed when their four-year-old daughter first ran out of the house to play with the other children, as though she were forsaking them.

THE NEED TO ESTABLISH
TRUST

For children to feel pleasure in trying to separate from their parents, instead of anger and guilt whenever this strong natural instinct is denied an outlet, the children need what Dr. David W. Winnicott, noted child psychiatrist, called a "good enough" mother to describe the less-than-perfect parent essential for healthy growth. Various terms have been applied to the feeling the child absorbs from the "good enough" mother, including what Winnicott describes as a "basic trust." Erik Erikson calls it an "inner certainty," and Dr. John Bowlby speaks of "secure attachment." All describe the child's relationship to the "good enough" mother as an emotionally secure base from which to move outward to explore the environment of first the home, and later the world.

Children denied this basic trust have little confidence in themselves or others. As siblings they try to keep their parents hovering over them, always near at hand to advise and make sure they do the right thing.

The most important experiences in a child's life occur with the mother and father during the earliest years. These experiences largely determine whether the child will grow up able to love others or will remain filled with hate; whether the child moves forward to meet life eagerly or is ridden with guilt over every step of growth, every move away from the parents; whether the child is cheerful or despairing, trusting or suspicious, confident or fearful, selfish or compassionate.

The "good enough" mother leads her child into the world of reality by encouraging, with smiles and kisses, exploration, staying behind except when needed. It is easy to understand what is needed for a child's physical development, but the requirements for emotional well-being are more complex. It is now becoming apparent through studies of parent-child relationships that the way in which the complicated and subtle emotional ties between child and parents are formed, or not formed, or broken, largely determines the way in which the child, as an adult, will make ties to those he or she loves or tries to love.

Despite the fact that the last several decades have been called the "age of the child" and the role of parents has been discussed and written about often, it is only in the last few years that the father has been considered important.

No one up to now has written about the "good enough" father, so let us make a start at considering what qualities he needs. He welcomes the idea of a child in the home and takes pleasure in the baby's conception. During the pregnancy, he identifies with the agony and ecstasy of his wife, shares the pains and pleasures of pregnancy with her. The "good enough" father is present at the birth of the baby, eager to hold the baby and bottle-feed it. He is prepared to diaper the infant, bathe the infant and be there as much as possible in the infant's life.

Recent research in infancy points out that babies are very much aware of the father in the first few months. Reuben Fine in *Narcissism, the Self and Society* gives evidence of the recognition of the father by the infant and the ease with which the infant relates to him.

The "good enough" father, together with his wife, offers consistent, tender love and care to the infant during the latter part of the first year, but more so in the second year when he helps in weaning and toilet-training.

The "good enough" father enjoys being a man and shows his children that he feels free to love a woman and accept her love. Many fathers could be "good enough" if they permitted themselves to express more openly their affection toward their wife and children.

The "good enough" father appreciates the uniqueness of his child, stressing his appreciation of his daughter's femininity and his son's masculinity. Such a father is interested not only in his child's achievements but can empathize with his child when he or she encounters the inevitable failures, losses, and defeats, and helps his child through them.

The "good enough" father is free to discuss sexuality as well as the whole range of human emotion, with his children. His own anger is at a minimum and his love at a maximum. He derives more pleasure than pain from living. He communicates with his children as much as possible and finds time to listen to them.

The "good enough" father is one who introduces his child to reality and lessens the child's attachment to the mother, helping the child gain sufficient autonomy and a sense of self-esteem.

Of course, the "good enough" father is itself an ideal, but, like all ideals, it is a worthwhile aim, whether partially or fully achieved.

WHEN LOVE IS MATURE

Studies of emotional development have given us a new idea of love. We now know that love does not suddenly erupt full-blown at adolescence, displaying itself in the passion of romantic ardor. Love is a developmental process that starts at birth and takes in many feelings over the years. The narcissistic love we feel as a child hopefully matures into a love that combines sexual desire with affection, tenderness, and respect. This love is possible when the man or woman, as a child, has felt affection, tenderness, and respect from his or her parents by touch, words, and actions.

If a mother and father are able to show tenderness, respect and affection for their children, they will also be able to allow each child to leave their sides and find his or her own way out of the room, out of the house, out of the family, when the child is ready. The child will not feel guilty at leaving the parents, but self-confident at being able to make the move away from them. Leaving is not an ending but a continuation. The child knows the parents are there if needed.

Siblings who are thus emotionally liberated no longer have to live out the dreams of their parents. They are free to live out their own dreams.

2

THE SIBLING:
A PARENT'S DREAM

THE POWER OF A PARENT

Each child is like a parent's dream. A dream contains the dreamer's wishes. Parents, like dreamers who shape their dreams, shape their children's lives in the image of their wishes.

In large part, parents create the personalities of the siblings they raise. The power of the parents and the innocence and vulnerability of the child make it inevitable that the early life of the child will be deeply affected by the behavior, expectations, and emotions of the parents.

Most parents are not aware of how they consciously and unconsciously build the lives of their children. Studies by prominent researchers in child development reveal that parents play out their conflicts through their children. Parents ask their children to live out their fantasies, and they assign different fantasies to each child. Parents determine what happens to a child, both physically and emotionally. One child is asked to fulfill the parent's frustrated desire to be a movie star or a rock singer. Another is asked to express the rebellion the parent never dared display. A third may be the focus of the parent's sexual desires, expressed subtly in ardent hugs and kisses. A parent may use one child as a whipping post, another as a hero or as a "savior" from the parent's depression. A parent may reward an inhibited sibling for restraining selfish and angry impulses—for example, giving chocolates to the "good" child who never loses his or her temper. Or a parent may unwittingly reward a child for stealing, behavior the parent consciously repudiates but unconsciously wishes to act out. Thus, parents assign various roles to different siblings, not always through words but through behavior, attitudes, and facial expressions.

At each stage of a child's development, parents relive their own childhood memories and emotions. They are reminded of the past, both the pleasurable and painful parts, by seeing it so clearly acted out by the child. Parents constantly reenact with their children, in an emotional sense, the script of their own lives. The siblings "catch," the contagion of the parent's fears and will fear the same things—sexual desires, expressions of anger, abandonment, or, in more concrete terms, perhaps thunder and lightning, illness, obesity, or failure in school.

We cannot emphasize too strongly that the parent becomes the child's role model. A child operates on the principle of "monkey see, monkey do." We might add "monkey senses, monkey reacts," because children are also affected by the more subtle influences a parent exerts on them. These influences go beyond copying a parent's behavior and sharing fantasies, dreams, and wishes. The child naturally starts to absorb the characteristics, actions, and attitudes of the parents, and may also act out the parents' hidden wishes without a word spoken between them.

Thus, siblings tend to carry out the secret mandates of their parents. How cooperative or competitive siblings are, how intellectual or athletic, how sensitive or insensitive, depends in large part on how they are molded by their parents.

THE PARENTS' RELATIONSHIPS

Much of what happens between siblings depends also on the emotional web of the family. Children reflect not only the relationship between them and their parents but also the relationship between their parents. This latter relationship is perhaps one of the most important issues in the sibling bond.

If a child watches parents solve their conflicts in a warm, loving way, negotiating their differences with a feeling of respect and concern for each other's point of view, the child will almost automatically assume this way of solving conflicts with others. But if the child witnesses parents in a continual battle, demeaning each other by name-calling, perhaps even striking each other, the child will emulate this aggressive way of handling conflicts. It is almost impossible for siblings to share warm, cooperative feelings when they live with parents who quarrel bitterly.

A husband and wife became alarmed because their seven-year-old son was constantly derogating his four-year-old sister. The fights became so intense that the parents sought out a therapist, who saw the mother and father, as well as the siblings, in family therapy sessions. As he listened to the little boy berate his sister with bitter, prolonged attacks, the therapist realized that the child was replicating the parents' behavior. The father verbally demeaned the mother just as the son demeaned his sister, and the mother responded as her daughter did with the same hurt and humiliated look.

However, while we continue to emphasize the importance of a warm, cooperative household as an important way to discourage siblings from fighting, we should remember that even the children of extremely cooperative parents need help in restraining themselves when in the grip of intense anger. Thus, the most loving, helpful parents who care deeply for each other and for their children will still have children who fight. When parents hear name-calling or see fist fights and angry faces they should accept the fighting as inevitable—but they should stop it.

THE PARENTS' FANTASIES

We do not wish to place blame in discussing how a parent may treat a child as a scapegoat or a saint and thereby set the standard of sibling behavior. All parents are unhappy, thoughtless, and selfish at times. But, only as parents understand the powerful part they play in forming their children's emotional outlook can they ease the suffering that has been handed down from parent to child probably since Adam and Eve.

Research on marital conflicts reveals that men and women tend to marry parts of themselves, either the idealized parts or the repudiated ones. A man who is inhibited and constricted is often attracted to a woman who acts more freely, who is openly affectionate, and more relaxed. Conversely, such a woman, perhaps a bit impulsive, often desires a mate who seems more controlled.

One wife said to a friend, with a sheepish grin, that she had never cursed until she met her husband. She added that he in turn cursed less than before they were married, out of deference to her. These traits became clear in the behavior of their two sons, one of whom was a habitual curser, while the other never used bad language. Parents often complain, I don't understand why one of my children is so well-behaved and the other is such a rebel. In fact, parents often unconsciously arrange for one part of their personality to be expressed by one child, another part by a second child.

A widower in his early fifties spoke to a friend because he was troubled by the behavior of one of his daughters. He had brought up the two daughters in the Jewish faith. One married a Jewish man, but the second was about to marry a man who was Presbyterian and slightly anti-Semitic. In talking to his friend, the widower learned an important fact about himself. There was a part of him that envied Gentiles. In fact, he realized, he had subtly encouraged his second daughter to seek friends who were not Jewish. Though he had asked his friend, "I tried my best to raise my daughters as Jews—why does one of them rebel against me?" he came to understand that his rebellious daughter was actually carrying out one of his deepest wishes.

It is difficult for parents to recognize their own contribution to a son's or daughter's rebellion. It is never easy, for example, for parents to acknowledge that when a child is warring with a schoolteacher or other authority the parents may derive some vicarious gratification. As difficult as it is to admit participation in a child's rebelliousness, however, this realization is probably the most important step in changing the child's behavior. When parents note consistently rebellious behavior in their child, whether within the sibling relationship or outside it, they should ask themselves, "What in my own personality is being gratified by this behavior?" Sometimes the answer does not come to mind immediately, but if the parents accept that they get some vicarious gratification from the child's rebellion, the answer will eventually come to light.

Ideal parents would like themselves, and therefore be able to spontaneously and intuitively help their children love themselves and each other. But, as we have said, many parents have difficulty liking themselves, and they may project their dislike onto their children, then expect the children to be perfect.

A successful businessman, in his youth, displayed a strong desire to please his mother and father, but secretly resented their many strict demands. Years later, he reenacted this early conflict with his own children. In his older son he fostered the kind of behavior that said: Be like me, obey all the rules, achieve as much as you can and never complain. This son turned into a quiet, law-abiding young man. In contrast, the businessman's younger son would scream when enraged, was often rebellious, and refused to carry out his parents' requests. He was revealing a part of his father's personality that the latter had unconsciously communicated to him. The father's strict conscience had always been in conflict with his wish to rebel. Each son showed a different side of his opposing wishes as each became an extension of his double personality. The older son was the "good" boy, the younger son the "bad" boy. It took the father some time in therapy to understand that the differences between his two sons, and the fights that often ensued between them, were reflections of a conflict in himself. He had been aware of his strong conscience, which his older son copied, almost caricatured, but unaware, at first, why his younger son had become a rebel.

This conflict between a parent's conscious wishes and his opposing hidden wishes from childhood often accounts for the vast differences among siblings. It is often said of siblings, "You wouldn't think they had the same parents!" But if the parents were closely examined, you would see that the siblings reflect different aspects of the parents—aspects of which both parents and siblings are not always aware.

A mother who came for therapy talked of the differences between her two teenage daughters. The older one was very repressed, kept to herself, and had few friends. The younger daughter, 15 years old, suddenly became promiscuous. The therapist wondered what accounted for such a vast difference between sisters only a year and a half apart. It became clear as the mother described her life. She was the daughter of an Episcopalian minister and a strict, religious mother. As a child, she had been taught to renounce all pleasure, to work hard at school and in the home, to go to bed early, never to disobey her mother or father. She had deeply resented the pressure placed on her to repress her sexual desires and need for romantic love.

Her daughters reflected the story of her inner and outer life. The older one was a mirror image of herself as the "good" girl. The younger one acted out the rebellious things her mother had wished to do as she subdued her emerging sexual passion.

Thus, many parents, perhaps all parents to some degree, arrange for their children to do what they wished they could have done in their youth but dared not out of fear of losing their parents' love and approval. Many an adolescent on drugs or alcohol, or living a free sexual life is unconsciously being aided and abetted by parents who vicariously, albeit unwittingly, are satisfying wishes they consciously deny.

3

My sibling,
my enemy

A NEW RIVAL

It is natural and normal for siblings to be rivals. The wish of every child is to be the sole recipient of the parents' love and attention. No child is free of sibling jealousy. As Hamlet said of Cain's act of murder, "It hath the primal eldest curse upon 't, /A brother's murder."

The child possesses the wish to be the favorite, the biggest, and the best, but a sibling always threatens this grandiose wish. The arrival of a newborn always imperils to some extent the older child's sense of omnipotence. One man recalled the arrival of his baby sister as "knocking me off my throne."

When parents accept the truth that every child wants the impossible—to be the most loved, the most praised, the most beautiful—and that sibling rivalry is normal in all families, parents can cope with it. No matter how kind, considerate, warm, and loving parents are, siblings will fight for the parents' love. In fact, rivalry is perhaps most intense when parents are understanding and lovable, as the children seek to be the favorite of such desirable parents.

As we have already pointed out, when parents can accept the absolute inevitability of rivalry between siblings without blaming themselves, they feel freer to settle sibling fights, to empathize with their children's natural competition, and to help them accept the need to curb their feelings of omnipotence. One of the reasons parents find it difficult to help siblings resolve their rivalry is that parents may unwittingly foster their children's wish to be all-powerful.

A mother brought her seven-year-old son for therapy, and when she realized how much he was helped, she became indignant because her daughter had been deprived of this benefit. She complained to the therapist, "If my son feels so good after seeing you, I insist his sister feel the same." She identified with her daughter and did not want her to be deprived of anything her brother received, though he was the one in need.

HELPING CHILDREN TO ACCEPT FRUSTRATION

Even though the above example is an exaggeration of a parent's wish to keep a child omnipotent, the wish exists in milder form in most households. To live peaceably with loved ones and friends, a child has to give up to some degree the idea of being the one and only. The child has to be able to feel: I am not entitled to everything all the time—all the food, all the toys, all the love. Many parents fail to help their children accept frustration and to curb their natural enmity toward each other.

Sibling rivalry can be tempered when the parents truly accept the notion that no child should have everything he or she wants at the moment it is demanded. A secure parent is able to give one child, who has already eaten lunch, ice cream d say to another who asks for it: You haven't had your meal and it will be better if you wait until after lunch to have t. This may be difficult for some parents because they secretly want their children's every wish to be granted, as they wanted the same thing when they were children.

Young siblings, especially preteens, are not yet able to view each other as individuals, each with needs, fears, and desires. They see each other in a distorted way—primarily as rivals. They misperceive each other's power and privileges. Most older siblings believe the younger ones are more admired and granted more favors, not realizing that the younger ones need more care.

Conversely, younger siblings believe the older ones have more privileges, which, of course, they do because they can take better care of themselves. Girls think brothers are treated as superior, brothers think their parents favor girls. We have never seen a boy or girl, man or woman, who, at one time or another, did not believe the psychic grass was greener on the sibling side of the fence.

Often, when siblings fight, they feel the other is loved, they are hated, the other is strong, they are weak. It is difficult when you are hungry to have only one slice of the pie—you want the whole. This grandiose hunger may cause deep unhappiness throughout life if the myth of omnipotence is not given up and moments of frustration are not accepted easily as part of growing up.

We have found that when parents can accept the fact that neither they nor their children can be gods, life becomes much more enjoyable for everybody. Marital and parent-child relationships, as well as sibling interactions, are all more harmonious when parents and children accept reality. Parents can still enjoy their own uniqueness and special talents and each child's uniqueness and special talents, providing that parents view themselves and their children realistically rather than through a haze of omnipotent fantasy.

HELPING SIBLINGS ACCEPT RIVALRY

A popular way siblings handle rivalry is by "squealing" on each other. They cry out, "That's unfair!" and run to the parent to protest angrily. This occurs particularly with children between six and ten years old. Behind squealing lies jealousy and envy. The accuser is charging: You have it all. I hate you for your greediness and I am going to try to stop you from enjoying it.

Sometimes parents identify with the one who squeals, who may be younger, and take away the privileges and pleasures of the older child. This helps neither child. Parents should talk things over with both siblings and help them live together more peacefully. Parents should assume the role of peacemaker rather than dictator, sympathize with each sibling, understand that age will make a difference. A four-year-old cannot accept as much frustration as a six-year-old. By the early teens siblings should be able to get along fairly easily.

Sometimes children and adults who experience strong sibling rivalry have the wish, usually quite strong, to become the other sibling. Many an unhappy boy who feels his mother and father favor a younger sister unconsciously tries to be her, while many an unhappy girl, who believes her brother is favored, tries to be him. This wish is not confined to opposite-sex siblings but also exists among siblings of the same sex. The older wishes to be the younger or vice versa.

Parents sometimes try to deal with this wish by accentuating the positive. They say to the envious child. "Look at all you have." This rarely works. When a child envies a sibling, or when any human being envies another, the child does not realize that the one envied never has it all. We distort the portion possessed by our rival, seeing, for instance, a small toy as an entire store of precious playthings.

A twelve-year-old boy who came for therapy envied an older brother, an expert in the sciences, an area in which the younger one had only limited ability. He constantly derided himself, saying over and over, I'm just a jerk. I wish I were brilliant like my brother—the older, overidealized brother who was perfect.

One day, the boy told his therapist a dream in which he appeared as Albert Einstein. He remarked wistfully, "There's the perfect scientist." The therapist said, "Are you aware that he was a very depressed man? He wore torn sweaters, hardly ever put on shoes."

The boy looked stunned, his hero gunned down by the revelation that the famed scientist did not care about himself enough to dress as others did but often resembled a child waiting for his mother to take care of him. The boy said, with a somewhat puzzled expression, "You mean Einstein and I are not that different? He had his quirks, too?"

The therapist was about to reinforce the boy's perception that he and his brother were not that different, that though his brother possessed certain skills he lacked, he had certain skills his brother lacked, when the boy remarked, "If Einstein had no shoes, there's a part of me that wants to be in his shoes." They both laughed. The boy was able to admit his rivalry with his brother and, once faced, it lost its power to make him feel so envious.

Parents should try to understand the feelings in a sibling that are often transformed into hostility and rage, and help the sibling to understand and control them. Parents should try to treat each sibling equally and understand the differences among the siblings without adding to the natural competitiveness. Parents should provide constructive outlets, such as encouraging one child to be artistic, another to collect stamps, a third to play tennis, a fourth to take up dancing, giving each child a "special" interest in which he or she can excel.

SEXUAL ATTRACTION AND SIBLING RIVALRY

There is one area of sibling rivalry we will deal with in more detail in a later chapter but that is worthy of mention here—sexual attractiveness. This wish to be the most sexually attractive sibling can lead to a rivalry many parents do not wish to notice and even therapists on occasion seem to forget. Because siblings of the same sex, or opposite sex, live so closely together, bathe together when small, undress and dress in front of each other, they are bound to be conscious of their bodies and to compete in sexual desirability.

In addition to the competition and envy, there is also the sexual attraction they feel for each other, both for the same sex when they are younger and for the opposite sex. Some of the wrestling between siblings shows a wish for bodily contact. Sometimes verbal attacks are actually disguised ways of expressing erotic feelings. Siblings may renounce their warm feelings for each other. Many a heated argument, or a fist-fight between siblings, is a defense—a way of warding off sexual feelings. A parent sensitive to the fact that siblings will naturally be attracted to each other—who else is nearest and dearest?—should say, I know it is difficult for you to express tender feelings for each other and that's why you fight. But try to understand the nice feelings. When this message is understood the anger and rivalry will recede.

Another dimension of sibling rivalry seldom understood is that siblings tend to project unacceptable parts of themselves onto each other. A boy who has the greedy wish to eat the entire chocolate cake turns on his younger sister and accuses, "You're a pig!" as he sees her take a second portion. An adolescent girl, frightened of her sexual fantasies about her brother, accuses her sister, "You dress like a sexpot!" The jealous siblings are accusing another sibling, "You're doing something I want to do, which I must deny because it is bad."

HOW PARENTS MAY CONTRIBUTE TO SIBLING RIVALRY

Sibling rivalry will probably remain a universal phenomenon as long as there are brothers and sisters. Accepting it as a reality will help parents to deal with its difficulties. Parents do not create it, though sometimes they can unwittingly intensify it. In Chapter 2 we saw how siblings follow the parents' model—copying their hostilities and reliving the parents' own unresolved sibling rivalries. For example, envy of one parent for the other, if intense, will incite similar envy and rage in siblings toward each other. If parents are constantly at war with each other, we can expect siblings to be at war with one another. Many parents say off-handedly of their screaming, fighting children, "Well, that's how children are." The parents do not realize that their own anger is being copied by the siblings. Constant sarcasm and tearing down of one parent by another, or of a sibling, will likewise increase hatred between siblings.

Conversely, if parents control their own hostility, the battle with siblings is more than half-won. If parents understand and subdue their own rage, their children will more easily understand and control theirs. Each sibling should be viewed by the parent as a person in his or her own right. No violence should be expressed between parent and child. If punishment is needed, it should not be physical punishment but the withholding of privileges.

A parent should not engage in a perennial battle with siblings, but rather guide the siblings through the difficulties they face in growing up. A child is far smaller and far less wise than a parent and is in need of love, protection, and support. The child who has a warm, generous, kind parent will not feel as an adult the loneliness of which so many people complain. The sibling whose parents help build self-confidence will later find that this inner strength will sustain the child when he or she leaves home.

If a parent has been hostile, however, either physically or emotionally, the sibling will later feel lonely even in the midst of friends or the intimacy of a close embrace, unconsciously longing for the parent of the past. Hostile parents create a tie between themselves and their children that is, perhaps, the hardest bond to break. For in hostility there is the touch, the feel of hand upon flesh, the intimate violation, so to speak, of the body. And to a deprived child any touch, whether tender or hurtful, is better than no touch at all, for the absence of touch is like death. The memory of a hostile touch remains a tie to the parent, a barrier in the way of establishing a close, enduring, loving relationship to another person.

TO HELP SIBLINGS BE INDEPENDENT

Parents need to allow each of their children to start achieving emotional separation from them. Only then will the siblings allow each other to have identities of their own and respect each other. Each sibling will, in this way, gain self-esteem and not vent anger and jealousy on other siblings.

Parents should help their children to separate from them

both physically and emotionally in a way that does not threaten or frighten the children. They should encourage the children's search for independence and stand by, ready to help if needed.

To some degree, all parents will experience a feeling of possessiveness about their children. After all, each child is their creation. But some parents have more difficulty than others in letting go of the child emotionally. In spite of their wish to love the child and do their best to care for him or her they do not understand that the child must achieve an independent spirit.

If parents find it difficult to permit a child sufficient independence they should try to determine what they may, unknowingly, be doing to discourage autonomy. Very often, parents who foster a clinging attitude in their children were victims of the same behavior from their parents. If they do not show the same attitude to their children, they may unconsciously feel they are being disloyal to their parents.

When separation and autonomy for a child become issues, the parent should ask, "What was my problem as a child when it came to separating emotionally from my parents?" If parents can acknowledge their own feelings, even at times in front of the children, they will feel freer to develop their independence. They sense the conflict anyhow, and when it comes out into the open they can deal with it far more effectively.

THE EXTREME
VULNERABILITY OF A CHILD

It is only within the last century that we have appreciated the vulnerability of children. In the past, children were viewed as miniature adults who had to be told what to do by parents who were always right. The complexity of the child's mind is now being appreciated. The experiences of our early, most vulnerable years, are far more powerful than most of us wish to believe. These experiences are the bedrock of our emotional development.

Children will be happier, and become happier adults, when parents understand how difficult it is to grow up. A part of the adult always yearns to remain a child. Many intense childhood fantasies have to be given up as unrealistic. If adults could more easily recognize the child in themselves, they would know their children better and help them more easily.

4

My sibling, my ally

M̲ost of the famous quotations about siblings written over
the centuries by poets, playwrights, and philosophers are in
praise of brothers and sisters. Thomas Carlyle wrote, "A mys-
tic bond of brotherhood makes all men one." Felicia Dorothea
Hemens wrote about a sibling, in the poem titled "The Child's
First Grief," the pleading lines, "Oh, call my brother back to
me!/ I cannot play alone." And Kipling, in "The Thousandth
Man," put it: "One man in a thousand Solomon says,/ Will
stick more close than a brother."

There are many advantages in being a sibling that the only
child will never know. Perhaps the most important is possessing a ready-made ally against warring parents or other children who act unfairly. The strong bond between siblings can
give much comfort when parents punish or when parents quarrel between themselves. Being a sibling is a captive relationship, but it also provides friends who serve as shields against

41

punitive parents and the sometimes terrifying world outside. Siblings offer a natural, near-at-hand love despite occasional ambivalent feelings.

Siblings also learn much from each other. They mutually acquire the ability to share, to trust, and to discover that they can be angry at someone their own age and still love them. This serves as a precursor for later relationships.

Also among the benefits of having a strong sibling bond is the feeling that one need not be a "loner," that one always has a friend, even though a friend with whom one fights at times. The only child has to learn second-hand from his neighbors—his pseudo-siblings—what it is like to have a friend. As one eight-year-old told a schoolmate in confidence, "I like you, but my sister is really my best friend."

HOW SIBLINGS HELP EACH OTHER

Siblings comfort each other in many ways, for instance when a parent is angry, depressed, alcoholic, or away on long trips. In an extreme situation, a sibling can come to the physical rescue of another sibling who is being harmed by a parent.

Siblings also help each other to accept frustration. An only child is apt to be indulged, but the child with siblings learns early that the world is not his or her oyster. Siblings accept sharing as a necessary part of living with others. Parents, however, must guard against asking younger children to deal with excessive frustrations before they are able to handle them.

An older sibling may assume a parental role, taking care of younger brothers and sisters. An older sibling may even try to replace a parent who is away much of the time or is emotionally remote, becoming a confidante to the other siblings. Siblings may give solace to each other in many ways. Sisters may become allies in homes where the boy "can do no wrong" and the sisters take all blame. Two siblings may comfort each other when a parent acts unfairly toward them, joining to fight the common enemy.

One brother and sister became close friends when he was ten and she was eight. They both sensed their mother was easily angered and prone to irritability. As each became a victim of her consistent wrath, they started to support each other against her; and the stronger their bond became, the less angry and provocative their mother was.

A middle child struck up a camaraderie with her younger brother as protection against an older brother who was a bully. Sometimes in this situation the third child becomes an outsider to the other two siblings.

Close relationships between siblings may create bonds so strong that they will be difficult to outgrow in later life. This, for example, is seen in unmarried sisters who remain together until they die. In the play *Toys in the Attic*, Lillian Hellman writes of an older sister who served all her life as caretaker for her brothers and sisters. She cries out at one point, "Why do I treat my mother's children as if they were my own?"

Siblings may experience a wide range of feelings for each other—from hatred to love. To be an ally, you have to feel more love than hate. But in our society, and perhaps in all cultures, sibling rivalry has tended to eclipse the love.

TO LOVE A SIBLING

To love consistently, whether the loved one is a sibling, a parent, or a friend, is a difficult task. In the process of growing up we all experience real and imagined frustrations and hurts, and cling to our hatreds and disappointments. To love consistently, a child has to traverse the stages of development with limited emotional scars.

In the Cradle

The capacity to form loving ties begins in the cradle. Authorities in child development have suggested some specific early experiences which are needed to produce men and women capable of giving and accepting love.

During the first stage of our development, what Erik Erikson has called the "trust-mistrust" stage and Freud the "oral" stage, we require consistent tenderness, love, and care. If this occurs, we develop an inner certainty and a sense of trust in the world around us.

The "Terrible Twos"

In the next stage, described by Erikson as the "autonomy versus shame and doubt" stage, the child requires a benign firmness, parents should set gentle but firm limitations. Freud called this the "anal" stage, referring to the emphasis on toilet-training, when the child is first asked to control a bodily function. This stage is also popularly called the "terrible twos" or the "no-no" stage as the child starts to exert his or her individuality. In this stage, parents should not be arbitrary but should help the child learn to control his impulses.

The reason this stage has been called the terrible twos is that it is a terrible time for many parents. Sometimes, parents fail to realize that children of this age are reluctant to give up the pleasures of doing what comes naturally. They resent using a toilet, as well as being the recipient of many dos and don'ts.

Parents need to be firm at this stage and not feel guilty when they are firm. Many power struggles that go on between parents and children are due to the fact that both parent and child are ambivalent about controlling the primitive impulses. The child wants to live exclusively according to the pleasure principle and feels angry when forced to abide by the dictates of reality. The parent feels guilty about saying no to the child.

Part of being a parent is saying "no" firmly and recognizing that even if the child objects, it is necessary to socialize the child. If the parent does not discipline the child, he or she will pay the penalty in later years when finding it difficult to make friends because of selfish behavior.

The way the parent says no to a child is important, because the child usually knows what the parent feels. Some parents say no but really mean yes; their manner is uncertain and their voice ambivalent, as in "maybe you'd better go to the bathroom now." Some parents are afraid the child will not love them even if they are asserting themselves on the child's behalf.

Then there is the parent who says no but with such an angry tone that the child rebels against the parent, feeling misunderstood and unloved. If the word no is to have an effect, it should be uttered with conviction, concern, and love.

The Family Romance

The third developmental stage, which Erikson calls "the initiative versus guilt" stage and which has also been referred to as the "family romance" stage, is a difficult time for most children. They are beset by erotic feelings for the parent of the opposite sex, and competitive feelings for the parent of the same sex. For children to emerge as loving people they have to be helped to tame their competitive drives and to modify their strong sensual feelings. No easy task, as those impulses are very strong ones.

This stage in a child's development often awakens some old conflicts in parents. Sometimes it is difficult for a father to see his son compete with him or for a mother to know that her daughter is competing with her. If parents were not permitted to experience competitive and lustful feelings as children, it is hard for them to accept these feelings in their own children. For parents to help children at this stage of life, they have to remind themselves that their sons and daughters are, by definition, competitive. Young people need help facing the fact that the wish for sex and the desire to be competitive are wishes that all human beings, perhaps all organisms in the animal kingdom, feel and want to gratify.

While we strongly urge that parents give their children permission to have sexual and competitive fantasies, we do not advise parents to endorse the acting out of these fantasies. Children have the right to feel and to spin fantasies, but not to act on them. For instance, the parental bedroom belongs to the parents, not the children. Parental dressing and undressing should be carried out in private. Too much stimulation is not beneficial for a child.

The Latency Period

Between the ages of six and ten, often referred to as the "latency" period, sexual feelings recede as the child learns family loyalty, values, a sense of fairness, and cooperation. This is the time when relationships within a family may change as each child seeks friends and develops new interests and skills. One child may deny an interest in drawing, for instance, if an older sibling has selected that area and shows ability in it. The younger one may be afraid to compete with a successful sibling.

Attending school and becoming a member of a group are powerful demands on a child this age. Many children feel aggressive, even cruel urges as they compete with peers, and resent the demands placed on them by adults. They call each other cheaters and squealers as they project their angry feelings, thus temporarily relieving them.

It is during the latency period that children need help becoming separate and autonomous. As we said before, when parents are not clinging to the images of their own parents, they are freer to give their children the autonomy and privacy the children need.

Adolescence

Adolescence is, as we all know from personal experience, a most difficult stage. Anna Freud called it "the normal psychosis" we all go through. We feel like an altruist one day, an egotist the next. A believer in free love on Monday and celibacy on Wednesday. Resolving ambivalence toward parents, developing an attitude toward sexuality, and attaining a realistic philosophy of life all are difficult tasks.

It is the rare child who makes the journey through these stages without conflicts. Every child, to some extent, feels some distrust toward parents, faces conflicts with autonomy, holds residues of ambivalence from the family romance, and finds it hard to always cooperate willingly and to face what adults call reality.

If a child were to pass through all these stages of development without much pain that child would come close to being what Dr. Reuben Fine has called the "analytic ideal." This child, as a young adult, would communicate a wide range of feelings with ease, would possess an enjoyable role within the family, express creativity, take pleasure in sexuality, have a strong sense of identity, and be free of neurotic symptoms.

For two or more siblings to consistently feel friendly and loving toward each other, they would have to be members of that exclusive and elusive club the "analytic ideal." There may be some honorary members, but I doubt if anyone has fully met all the qualifications. Consistent love is a rare, if not impossible achievement. It requires a psychic Hercules.

HOW PARENTS CAN HELP
SIBLINGS BECOME ALLIES

Let us see what happens between siblings at each stage of development, note the difficulties, and show how parents can help their children to love each other better and to become stronger allies.

Rivalry During Infancy

In the first year of life, each child wants to be, as we have stressed, the center of attention. If a rival sibling enters the scene when the first baby is still suckling—eleven or twelve months old—this becomes a trauma for the first-born. Even if the older child does not yet talk, the child protests by cries and screams or by angry, unhappy expressions.

When the older child is only a year old, parents want to protect the older child's pride, and yet must take full care of the new baby. It is a difficult time for parents. Most new parents feel overwhelmed, and it is the rare parent who can relax and enjoy two infant children. It is natural for siblings a year apart to hate each other, because their needs are so similar and they resent the parental demands to share and cooperate.

But it is possible for two siblings no more than a year apart to love each other, though for this to take place parents have to be aware of the inevitable resentments both children are bound to experience and not to feel defensive. The parent who wants to help siblings love each other has to feel free to say in essence to each child: I know you'd like to have it all and you feel angry when your new sibling gets something. But you can't have it all. You have to learn to share. If parents can get across this idea, their children will start to cooperate as a way of life. They will become less selfish, beginning a mutual friendship.

To get any idea across to their children, parents must believe it themselves. When a parent says, "You can't have it all, you must learn to share with your brother and sister," the parent must have the conviction that this is the way life should be. Frequently, when a child is not sharing with the sibling, despite the parents' instructions, the child senses that the parent has rejected the idea that sharing is a valuable act. Usually, when a parent is unwittingly rejecting the notion of sharing, the parent is unconsciously resenting the sharing he or she was forced to do with siblings. On some level, the parent wants the child, in spite of siblings, to have it all, as the parent did not.

When a child is immersed in the toilet-training phase and is angry at the restraints being placed on him or her, the advent of a sibling is experienced as another heavy emotional load to bear. The child habitually saying "no-no" during the "terrible twos" will by nature say "no" to the birth of a rival. It is important to realize that how siblings view each other depends on the stage of development at which the older one first meets the younger. Parents need to recognize the natural resentment of a child when blessed—to the child, cursed—with a new sister or brother. Parents need to acknowledge, in their behavior and attitudes, that they understand how much the birth of a brother or sister will be resented by a two-year-old. It is not uncommon for the latter to want to grab a hammer and hit the newborn rival over the head.

A two-and-a-half-year-old boy, born with a slight fracture on his head but nurtured so beneficently by both parents that he became a "darling" of a child, at the birth of a sister fought toilet-training, screamed when his mother or father set any limits, and looked daggers at the new arrival. One day, he told his parents he was going to take a hammer and strike the baby "right on the head," referring to the fracture and the hurt he had suffered earlier. He wanted to inflict on his new rival the specific pain he felt had been inflicted on him.

The Need for Rules During the "Terrible Twos"

Parents tend to vacillate with two-year-olds, either becoming too angry and restrictive or too indulgent, or swinging between the two extremes. Many parents need help saying "no" to their children, and usually the most difficult time is during the terrible twos. Parents become angry when children defy them, and they tend to fight back. But perhaps even more parents feel so frightened of their child's aggression, and their own anger, that they become inhibited and fail the child by not setting consistent limits.

The two-year-old needs to know that there are rules and that the parent means business if the child does not honor them. Parents should not act like ogres, however, but warm, benign limit-setters and protectors. When a two-year-old realizes his or her parents are saying that the younger rival is here to stay but that the older child also has a rightful place in the family, hatred tends to diminish toward the younger sibling.

All two-year-olds want to regress and become the "baby," and parents should recognize this as a normal wish but not indulge it. If the wish is indulged, the two-year-old will become a competitor rather than an ally or protector of the new baby. The older child can be taught to enjoy giving the baby a bottle, to help assist a parent to hold the baby, and to tuck the baby in at night.

When parents find themselves upset about their two-year-old not wanting the newborn sibling around and are frightened by the two-year-old's temper tantrums, they can reduce their discomfort by asking themselves, What is really upsetting me about these angry thoughts and feelings and acts? Usually, when a parent is disturbed at a child's vituperative displays, the parent, as a child, has been told never to feel angry or think angry thoughts, or dare to act on anger.

Such a parent needs help in recognizing that no child in the world welcomes a newcomer one hundred percent. Anger is inevitable, and the older child needs help in verbalizing this anger. It is calming to a two-year-old who resents a newborn sister or brother to hear a parent say, "It was great, wasn't it, being all alone, and it's hard in many ways to have a new sibling. If you feel angry, tell me about it. I understand."

A Second Trying Time

When a child between the ages of three and six becomes a big brother or sister, this is also a trying time. The child is now caught in the family romance conflict, wishing to be the spouse of the parent of the opposite sex and to do away with the parent of the same sex. Children express this wish along these lines: "I want to marry my mother (or father) and have a baby with her (or him). I'm angry at Mommy and Daddy for having that baby together."

The girl child wants to be the mother of the new baby, not

the sister. Children of this age feel like losers as they fail to gratify the universal fantasy of wedding the parent of the opposite sex and having a child with that parent. Thus do we prepare at an early age for the passions that will later take us through marriage and parenthood.

Children play house at this time, and try to be the mother or father of the sibling or of a substitute, such as a cat or puppy. It is painful for these children to observe their parents in the driver's seat while they sit silently in the back, their wishes frustrated.

For children to move from a state of hating to a state of loving their siblings, parents have to recognize the dilemma of the Oedipal child. They should let their children know they are aware of the natural wish, at this time, to be married and to become a parent. But just telling a child once that the parent is aware of this disappointment does not resolve the problem, it is only a beginning.

We shall never forget the haunting words of a five-year-old girl in therapy who, after the birth of a sister, threw temper tantrums, raged at the new baby, and wanted to get into bed with her father at night and throw her mother out of the room. During her therapeutic play, she pretended she was the mother and the therapist was the father of her new baby. He encouraged her to talk and to play out her fantasies. In the process, she started to lose her anger at her mother and father for having the baby. But the therapist knew that she had to accept the fact that, as a five-year-old, she could not be a wife or mother. The therapist explained at least twenty times that while she wanted to marry and have a baby, she was not ready for this at her age. She would have to wait until she was older and could find a suitable man. On hearing this, she looked at the therapist sadly and said, "It's so hard to wait."

Children find it hard to wait for the fulfillment of any wish. This little girl later consulted the same therapist when she was twenty-six and unable to settle down with one man. She was still holding onto the fantasy of marrying a father figure. She needed further help in taming her wish to be her father's wife and to have a baby with him. The second time round in therapy was successful, and a year after she ended therapy, the therapist received notice of her wedding.

One of the reasons Oedipal wishes are hard to give up is that all children, as well as most adults, have powerful omnipotent fantasies that are rarely faced or discussed. Though the Greek tragedy of Oedipus is thousands of years old, it persists in literature because it stirs fantasies in every man, woman, and child. No one is immune, as a child, from the natural desire to passionately love the parent of the opposite sex. No one is immune from wanting it all, and even though we know better when we grow up we still often cling to the wish. To help children renounce their unrealistic wishes adults need to tame their own. This is another example of what we said earlier—to get children to do what will make them happier in the long run, if not at the moment, parents must have the conviction that it is indeed the right thing to do.

As Children Move Away from Parents

During the latency period of six to 10 years of age, children should start moving away from parents and join the world of their peers. This is a tough time, too (no time is easy during childhood), because many demands are placed on the child all at once. The child has to attend school and sit quietly all day, instead of moving freely around the home as before. The child has to share a teacher with many peers, instead of getting all the attention. Also, the child must become a worker, no longer a lily of the field.

At this stage there are similarities to the previous period. Children resent restrictions, they still yearn to be self-centered and have demands fulfilled immediately. When a child this age is given too many responsibilities—music lessons, boy scout or girl scout membership, church or synagogue attendance, sports, informal clubs with peers—the child often resents the privileges and pleasures he or she believes a newborn possesses. We have noticed how many latency children want to regress to earlier stages of development because of pressures they cannot handle. More youngsters this age are treated in child-guidance clinics than at any other age, as the advent of a sibling intensifies their anger and heightens their wish to be treated like the new baby.

It takes a great deal of patience on the part of parents to meet with the onslaughts of a latency child who frequently resents the seemingly regal position of a suckling brother or sister. But, if parents accept normal sibling resentments, they can show their latency child some of the pleasures of being a big brother or sister, for example, the role of a protector and guide to the pleasures life offers.

One eleven-year-old girl could not wait to show her year-old sister the wonders of nature. When her little sister could walk, she took her by the hand and led her down the street showing her the varieties of flowers in the neighbors' yards and the different kinds of trees along the way. She also took her sister on her first visit to a beach, held her hand as she led her slowly toward the water and into it up to her knees, observing the happy, almost blissful look on the baby's face.

The Adolescent Sibling as Ally

During adolescence, when a boy or girl is able biologically to become a parent and has conscious fantasies of being one, the birth of a brother or sister can be quite traumatic for at least two reasons. The first is because the adolescent feels extremely jealous of parents conceiving a baby at a time the adolescent could be a parent.

The second reason, an issue rarely recognized, is that during adolescence, with all the biological changes that take place, sensuous desires become very intense. A teenager feels, in certain ways, more dependent than ever and retreats in fear from strong desires. We see this in an adolescent's extreme hunger for food, either binging excessively or denying the hunger and starving. The adolescent cannot cope with strong dependency wishes, for they are too threatening. Adolescence is a difficult period because on the one hand appetites are stimulated more than ever, but on the other hand the adolescent may be terrified of these appetites and try to curb them. Thus, we see many teenagers going from anorexia to bulimia, from sexual promiscuity to celibacy.

When the adolescent sees a new baby in the home this situation presents a difficult dilemma. The adolescent would love to be that baby once again, but must repudiate this dependency desire. Because the adolescent's dependency wishes are intensified at this time, to watch a new baby receive the parents' love is bound to be upsetting.

This issue is often overlooked because few parents recognize the strong dependent yearnings that still exist in adolescents. Parents tend to think of an adolescent as an independent adult. But no adolescent is. It takes awareness on the part of a parent to reassure an adolescent, "In certain ways we all want to remain a baby cared for by the mother. I sometimes want to be. Maybe you do, too. Don't feel ashamed. It's a universal wish." By becoming aware of these feelings and knowing they are natural, not abnormal, the adolescent can then cope with them, gradually accept them and control them, instead of fighting them, and feeling angry and guilty. We all want to be reassured that the very wishes for which we feel the most guilt are wishes everyone possesses, that we are not freaks or crazy because such wishes come to mind.

The Younger Child's Point of View

These then are the ways in which a younger sibling's birth may affect an older sibling. But the younger sibling will also react differently to the older sibling, depending on the younger child's stage of development. In the first year, a child still expects things immediately, and as the child becomes aware of the existence of an older sibling, the child feels frustration at having to share the parents' love. A younger sibling also feels pressure to accomplish tasks prematurely because the older sibling is doing things the child cannot yet do.

Parents should recognize that when a younger sibling is going through toilet-training he or she may feel angry and jealous of the older child's achievements in this area. Parents should allow the younger child to make mistakes, have accidents, just as the older sibling once did, just as the parents themselves did as children.

A two-and-a-half-year-old boy who had a brother three years older was brought for therapy because he suffered from insomnia, was phobic about leaving the house, and seemed constricted in expressing his feelings. The therapist sensed that the boy felt a pressure to accomplish tasks too quickly. In play therapy, the therapist kept the pressure low. The therapist was pleased one day when the boy asked, "Do pencils have erasers because we all make mistakes and have accidents?" The therapist reassured him that this was the reason for erasers and the boy looked content.

Often a child in the Oedipal stage turns to an older brother or sister and acts out the Oedipal conflict with the sibling. Many a younger sister wants to marry an older brother, or a younger brother wishes to marry his older sister. These wishes between siblings are inevitable, and parents should not act punitively when the wishes surface.

A latency youngster may resent an older sibling because the child views the sibling as similar to a parent—an older person who restricts the child and makes demands. Many an older sibling does become demanding and controlling of a younger one, usually copying a parent's behavior. As a matter of fact, we have rarely seen a consistent conflict in a sibling that has not been consciously or unconsciously fostered by the parents. A part of the parent unconsciously arranges for the children to become who they are. When siblings are loving allies, it is generally because the parents want them to be loving allies. When children are hateful, parents have to face their own feelings and ask, "What am I doing that is aiding in my children the very things I repudiate consciously?" Parents can best help their children become allies by being allies themselves, a state that unfortunately does not occur often enough in these days of high divorce and separation rates.

"YOU'VE GOT TO BE TAUGHT TO HATE"

Parents are every child's first teachers. As the line from *South Pacific* goes, "You've got to be taught to hate." When children see their mother and father greeting each other lovingly, solving problems reasonably, and respecting each other, the children emulate this behavior. But, if parents fight and threaten each other, then siblings view each other as threats and will fight among themselves.

It is true that siblings can become allies when they have one or both parents as a common enemy. But, when people are allies because of a common enemy they are also taught to hate, since the hate in large part unites them. As adults, such children will continue looking for both allies and enemies, repeating the family pattern.

For a sibling to be a genuine ally, he or she has to experience a loving relationship with both parents. Our culture has often been referred to as a "hate" culture. Individuals compete more often than they praise. They feel jealousy more often than they feel empathy. They demean others and themselves more often than they encourage and compliment. It should not surprise us therefore that the professional and nonprofessional literature on childraising focuses more often on sibling rivalry than on sibling love.

It is often asked if the number of siblings affects how much love a mother and father can give, since the more siblings, the greater the competition for the parents' love. But if the relationship between the mother and father is warm and loving, and they are reasonably firm with their children when necessary, there is enough love for every child. The parent will have little need to favor one over the other, as he or she will empathize with each child.

It is not easy, physically or emotionally, being a mother or father, especially to a new baby. It means sleepless nights when the baby cries. It means endless feeding and teaching the child to eat. It means spending time with the child when the parents are exhausted or just want to relax. It means expending endless energy dressing the child, keeping him or her clean. It takes an exceptionally even disposition not to become irritable or to have moments when the parent wishes the child had never been born. No matter how loving and easygoing a parent is, no one is perfect. No parent can be caring all the time, a parent will naturally feel ambivalent at times.

But if parents can accept this ambivalence, know they are entitled to it, they will have more moments for love and for understanding their children, moments that will increase the children's ability to be good friends with each other as they grow up.

Kurt Lewin, a social psychologist, has studied various forms of leadership with groups of children. He divided the types of leadership into "authoritarian," "laissez-faire," and "democratic." He found that under authoritarian leadership the children complied with the leader's demands, but then showed anger and inhibitions in their behavior. Under "laissez-faire" leadership the children could come and go as they pleased and were frequently indulged but not guided, their competitiveness was strong, enmity greater toward each other, and they showed little pleasure in personal relationships. Under "democratic" leadership, the children obeyed the reasonable requests, showed much pleasure in each other as well as in the leader and, in contrast to the other two groups, got along well with each other when the leader was absent.

This study has important applications to child-rearing. It suggests that parents who are too restrictive encourage resentment in children, who then fight with each other. It also suggests that those parents who are too indulgent and who fail to guide children do not help them to love each other or themselves, whereas reasonable, democratic parents help their children get along with each other both while the parents are present and in their absence. This also increases self-esteem in their children.

We can teach siblings to become loving allies. A sibling who has received a fairly secure emotional foundation as an infant and young child can love his or her siblings much of the time. Siblings cannot always be loving, but they can be aware that when they feel anger they need not always express it and that sometimes anger is justified but at other times has no real basis.

As we look at siblings, we see that, in the long run, as they grow up they are often of inestimable help to each other in easing both the small traumas of everyday life and the mammoth traumas that occur when there is separation or death in the family. One sibling may serve as haven for another sibling as they ride out the emotional storms together.

5

WHEN THERE
ARE TWO SIBLINGS

THE NUMBER OF SIBLINGS
IS NO ACCIDENT

The number of siblings in a family is, by and large, no accident. The actual number of siblings in a family is arranged, unconsciously, by the parents for the most part. The number is determined by the parents' wishes, hopes, and fantasies. Parents usually have both conscious and unconscious motives that explain how large a family they wish to produce. We have mused, at times, about the paradox of parents who can afford to have many children raising few, while parents who have little money often raise many children.

The number of children in a family is usually related to the parents' emotional experiences as children and to the size of the family in which they grew up. Most parents have at least the same number of children as in their original families. In many instances both husband and wife were one of two children and wanted three of their own. It seems that when people become parents, they often want to go their parents one better—and the size of a family is often influenced by this desire.

There are exceptions to this rule. If, in a two-sibling family, a parent has an older brother or sister whom he or she disliked, the wish is strong to have only one child, representing the parent minus the obnoxious sibling. Or, if a parent comes from a large family, he or she may want only one child, having wished to be an only child.

One woman, the youngest of thirteen children who lived on a farm, married a man, the youngest of six siblings. By unconscious mutual consent, they had only one child. Neither wanted their children to suffer, as they felt they had suffered, from lack of attention. The mother told a close friend, "I grew up practically unnoticed by my mother and father and brothers and sisters. My best friend was Flossie, my cat." The father also wanted to spare his children what he felt had been ostracism by his older siblings.

Thus, the size of a family is usually related, to some extent, to how parents fared in their families and how they viewed their own siblings. When parents plan to increase the size of their families it is helpful to them and their future offspring to review with each other how they felt in their own families. Did they resent being the oldest child? Did they feel scapegoated as the youngest child? Did they feel caught in the middle?

Frequently, persons who marry find themselves feeling quite similarly about family size. Many times, when a man and woman marry they secretly hope to remedy old hurts. When the marriage does not provide sufficient remedy, couples often think of having more children. The reason it is helpful for prospective parents to discuss why they want a second or third child is that they may uncover some unrealistic expectations. They may, for example, realize they are trying to use a child to save a marriage or to compensate for feelings of inferiority or loneliness.

When these irrational wishes are faced, they lose their power, and parents can then decide more realistically whether they shall increase the size of the family. Getting in touch with unrealistic wishes in no way implies that parents should not have more children. Rather, we suggest that a discussion of the parents' pasts, particularly how they felt as siblings, can strengthen them and help them feel more competent in the parental role.

WHY PEOPLE BECOME PARENTS

Just as there are a host of reasons why parents have a certain number of children there are a host of reasons why people become parents in the first place.

One reason men and women have children is that ever since the start of recorded time there has been social pressure to do so. The Bible says, "Be fruitful and multiply." This admonition becomes part of our conscience and we may feel either guilty or incomplete if we do not obey it. Very often, the guilt becomes reinforced when families and friends ask accusingly of a childless couple, Is something wrong?

Another reason people have children is that when a man and woman establish a loving relationship they want to have as much in common as possible. When a child is born, both parents recognize a part of themselves in the features of the child, as well as a part of the partner. This is as close as they can get to sharing something priceless, and the bond can help perpetuate the intimate relationship.

Having a child also offers reassurance to the parents regarding their sexual identity. They feel more a man or a woman. Women are proud to show their pregnant bodies to others. And just as women feel more feminine, men feel more masculine and celebrate paternity by handing out cigars.

But the most fundamental reason for having a child is that the child increases the parents' self-esteem. If there is any doubt about this, become a coach of a Little League baseball team. Here you find parents competing with each other from the stands, projecting their narcissism onto their children, screaming for their children's team to win. Parents' narcissism can also be observed when someone praises their children.

Most parents then smile as though they were being praised themselves. Or, if their children are criticized, the parents cringe. Parents want children to have high marks not always for the children's sake but for the parents', as though the praise were a tribute to the parents for producing such brilliant children.

Such narcissistic investment by parents in their children affects the children. If narcissistic wishes arouse a strong desire for achievement, parents will push their children to compete excessively and to achieve persistently. If parents are fortunate enough to possess a healthy self-esteem—a mature narcissism, rather than a childish narcissism—they will foster cooperation and love in their children.

WHAT IT IS LIKE TO BE ONE OF TWO SIBLINGS

There are unique features of sibling interaction when there are only two siblings—brother and sister, brother and brother, or sister and sister. How two siblings get along is dependent on many factors. One is the age difference. Siblings, for instance, who are separated by ten years will have a closer community of interests than either one has with an adult. But their ease in communicating, empathizing, and identifying with each other is not nearly as great as with those siblings closer in years. The latter play, argue, love, and compete in a more evenly-matched manner than a younger and an older sibling.

If a child is only one year or one and a half years old when a sibling is born, the rivalrous feelings of the older child will be strong at first, resenting the birth of the newcomer. A young child often senses the resentment of the older sibling and makes various accommodations. The child may submit, withdraw, fight back, or, in some cases, learn to cooperate.

When the older child is two or three years old at the sibling's birth and has received constant affection and attention from parents, resentment at the newcomer is usually less. How the child experiences the newborn depends on where the older child is in physical and emotional development. If the older child is undergoing toilet-training, he or she will resent the newborn's freedom to excrete whenever and wherever the baby wishes. This explains why so many older siblings, upon the birth of another child, will act as though they have forgotten their toilet-training. They may even regress as far back as asking to be fed from a bottle again.

If the older sibling is four or five years old and starting to experience sexual fantasies, the child may fantasize the new baby as his or her own child. This wish may become more intense the older the sibling is. If the sibling is eight or nine years old, he or she may try to turn the new baby into his or her own. It is not uncommon for a younger child to inadvertently call an older sibling mommy or daddy. One girl of eleven, when her mother gave birth said to her grandmother, "This is my baby, it belongs to me." She treated the baby as though it were her own, hugging it close and demanding that she feed the baby, cover her up, and put her to sleep. If the older child becomes the caretaker, he or she may influence the relationship between the two siblings by affording the younger one an extra protective arm.

When two siblings are near in age, they may work overtime to make their parents feel they are each special. Because the rivalry is more acute than if there were more years between them, it is difficult for them to say, I love my brother or I love my sister.

A question many parents ask is: When is it best to have a second child? The best answer is: When you both feel comfortable about the idea. From the children's point of view, when they are three or more years apart they are more likely to cooperate, but there are so many variables that influence the sibling relationship that this, too, varies.

The most opportune time for parents to have another child is when the tensions between parents are limited and the pleasures are many. A child rarely, if ever, improves a marital relationship. If there are tensions between the parents they should be faced either through conversation and negotiation or, if necessary, through marital counseling. Only when parents feel essentially happy can they rear happy children. Also, parents should feel secure with the children they already have. Just as a marriage is rarely improved by increasing the size of the family, a parent-child relationship is rarely improved by having more children.

Perhaps more crucial than age differences between siblings is the parent's sense of ease when they see them together. If two siblings play happily and there is a look of pleasure on the parents' faces, the siblings will probably take this as approval and continue to enjoy their own company. But if parents show disapproval or anxiety, the siblings may reflect this discomfort and start to quarrel with each other.

It is important for parents to convey how much each child means to them. Parents unwittingly project parts of themselves onto their children, and if parents become aware of this they are able to see their children more as individuals, rather than their fantasied projections. Parents may try to turn their children into their own siblings. To parents, one child may represent himself or herself while another child may stand for either a hated or loved sibling.

A mother and father may have varying perceptions of the same child because of their different past experiences. A sibling may become confused when the mother's and father's views are different and they argue about the child's behavior. Parents have to beware of reliving their past difficulties and failing to see their children as unique human beings. There is often a great temptation for parents to do this, but it is never helpful to the children. Remember, parents in many ways set the stage for the dramas that transpire between their children. How cooperative or competitive siblings are, how loving or hateful, will depend in large part on how much both parents believe in cooperation over competition and in love over hatred.

Just as parents should talk over their wishes when they consider increasing their family, it is frequently helpful for parents to discuss who their children remind them of. For example, if a daughter reminds a father of a beloved sister while she reminds the mother of a hated sister, these memories may seriously interfere not only with the parent's relationship with the daughter but with the marriage itself. Parents should try to look at a child not as a sibling, but as a child in the present, an individual in his or her own right.

TWO ARE MORE INTIMATE
THAN THREE OR MORE

Parents should realize that there is likely to be a more intense relationship between two siblings than among three or more. Two siblings have to deal with each other over more hours and in a more intimate way. Two siblings stand by themselves, vie with each other head-to-head for parental love. There is always a tendency, no matter how many children, to compete and to compare the amount of love given by the parent. When there is only one peer present, rather than two or three, the tendency becomes stronger. This intensity also applies to other areas. There is generally more sex play and more hostility between siblings when there are only two. Both sexual drive and hostility seem to dilute in larger families.

Parents should not be upset when they see acute rivalry between two siblings. The younger child will always resent the power and the privileges accorded the older child, whereas the older one will always think of the younger one as more loved, more sheltered, more indulged, and enjoying an easier life. This makes their rivalry run deep.

Because two siblings tend to vie for attention more than several siblings do, parents may need to help them limit this competition. One father played touch football with his two sons, but frequently played against the two to encourage them to cooperate as a team. In another family, which was accustomed to dining out every Sunday night, the daughter was asked to choose the restaurant one week, the son the next.

Many parents in two-child families have noticed that the second child is often more relaxed, easier to cope with, and less troublesome to the parents. Though there are constitutional differences between children, we think the oft-repeated observation that the youngest child is less worrisome occurs because first-time parents are apt to be more nervous and less competent. Veteran parents are not as filled with anxiety by the time the second child arrives.

PREPARING THE OLDER SIBLING FOR THE NEW ARRIVAL

Parents should prepare the older child for the arrival of the younger sibling, recognizing the inevitable anger and telling the child that they will continue to love him or her just as much as they always have. Parents should also stress that the newcomer will need much care, just as the older child needed it when a baby. Parents should also take a certain degree of jealousy and rivalry for granted and not be upset by it. They can easily handle it if the residue of their own sibling rivalry is not too intense.

As in any form of learning, a child needs more than one lesson to be prepared for the arrival of a sibling. Rather, questions probably will arise, sometimes in disguised form, several times a week. In preparing a child for the advent of a sibling it is important for parents to realize that the older sibling will feel concerned about being supplanted and will be worried about future status. The older sibling will undoubtedly wonder if the parents' love will be lost forever because of the newcomer.

These concerns cannot be taken care of by one or two reassuring comments. When the child recognizes that the parents are spending a lot of time talking about a future brother or sister—the times when the newcomer will be resented, and the times when the older sibling will be admired and loved by the newborn—the child will feel more relaxed.

The parents also might point out that, as children, they resented newcomers in their lives and suggest that the child talk to them when feeling angry or disturbed in any way and that they will try to help him or her understand these feelings. As we have just pointed out, parents usually find themselves more relaxed with the second child, so they can afford to spend time with their first-born and reassure the older child that he or she will not lose the place in their hearts.

With the second and all subsequent siblings, parents get a chance to learn more about bringing up a child. The first sibling may suffer more than the others because this child is, in many ways, an experiment. However, to make up for the suffering, the first child enjoys the privilege of being the only child who, at least for a while, possesses the parents all to himself or herself.

Gender may make a difference, in that a boy may become allies with a younger sister but feel rivalrous with a younger brother. Conversely, a boy may think a sister gets more attention and love. Or a girl may believe her brother is favored because he is stronger, even though she is older and thinks she should come first.

TRY NOT TO FAVOR EITHER CHILD

It may become a hardship for the other child when one is favored by a parent. Parents have a tendency to compare and contrast two children, particularly when one is a girl, the other a boy. It is devastating to a child when a parent asks bitterly, "Why aren't you more like your brother (or sister)?" This says to the child, "I hate you, I love your sibling."

One of the cruelest remarks ever made to a child was uttered by a mother after she learned that her older son had been killed in a car accident. She wailed to her younger son and daughter, "Why couldn't it have been one of you?" They, of course, had sensed over the years that he had been her favorite, but it increased their pain to hear her say she wished one of them had died instead of her beloved oldest son. Such a preference, in fact, was the basis of the book and movie *Ordinary People*.

If parents can be more aware of their biases, including their preference of one gender over another, they would indulge in less favoritism and all their children would grow up feeling more emotionally secure, more loved, and more loving. The pain of preference, suffered by the one not preferred, holds special agony for a child.

When parents find themselves feeling unduly biased in favor of one child, one of two things is usually occurring: either they are reliving part of their past and resenting the child who reminds them of a hated brother or sister, or the child reminds the parent of a hated part of himself or herself.

It is not easy to give up past resentments, when one felt victimized by an older brother or sister. But a parent has to separate his or her sibling from the child in the present. Often, a parent holding onto resentments toward a sibling makes his or her own child more powerful, important, and grandiose than the child really is. If a parent can realize this, he or she will resent the child less and is less apt to play the game of favorites.

Parents often hate in their child what they hate in themselves. If parents find themselves disliking a certain quality in their child they should ask themselves: Does this quality exist in me? One father found himself resenting his son's shyness and desire to be alone. When the father could acknowledge that he had the same wishes at times, and felt selfish and guilty for having them, he was able to understand his son's wish for occasional solitude.

Often, favoritism has to do with the gender of a child. We all grow up feeling the other child has it better; boys think girls are favored and girls think boys are. To accept sons as boys and daughters as girls, parents have to be secure in themselves and their own sexual identity. If they find they are playing favorites by liking a daughter, for instance, over a son, they have to ask themselves: What don't we really accept about our own gender?

For two siblings to cooperate with ease each needs to feel unique. For this reason, it is a good idea to give each sibling a separate bedroom, toys, and clothes. Hand-me-downs may save money, but they frequently incur an emotional expense of resentment in the younger child, who feels less preferred. When two children continually ask parents, directly and indirectly: Who do you like better? parents know their children do not feel secure but sense parental favoritism.

Few parents will be so insensitive as to say that they prefer one child over the other to the degree that they would sacrifice one child for the other. But the answer: I love you both the same, does not seem to satisfy siblings. Why? Because each wants to be loved more. Parents will find it easier to tell each child that they understand that the child would like to be loved more than the other siblings. Parents should let the children, when they ask such a question, talk on, because usually the children's own distortions will become clear.

When five-year-old Judy asked her mother and father, "Do you love me better than you love Jimmy?" who had been born just a year before, the parents started a frank discussion with her over the similarities and differences between boys and girls. At one point Judy asked her father wistfully, "Do you like boys better than girls?"

He assured her, "I love you because you are you, not only because you are a girl. And I love Jimmy because he is Jimmy, not only because he is a boy." Children should feel loved for who they are—including their gender. This discussion proved beneficial to Judy, allaying her fears, and to her mother and father who felt they had helped her feel more secure.

A question from a child usually holds a hidden meaning. It is this meaning that parents should encourage children to discuss. Judy was saying she thought her father preferred her brother because he was a boy. Her father was able to correct her distortion.

Most parents would like their two children to love each other and to cooperate perfectly. However, this is asking too much from both parents and children. Life is never perfect, and when there are two siblings, one will always feel the other's existence creates certain frustrations and dissatisfactions. Parents have to recognize this fact within their children and within themselves. When parents accept each other easily, with little frustration and dissatisfaction, their children will copy this attitude. Then each child will accept a sibling's existence with less resentment and anger.

6

WHEN THERE ARE THREE OR MORE SIBLINGS

ADVANTAGES AND DISADVANTAGES OF A LARGE FAMILY

Some psychologists believe that much of our character and behavior are influenced by our "ordinal pattern"—whether we are the oldest or the youngest child, or somewhere in the middle. Dr. Alfred Adler, a prominent psychologist of the early 1930s, pointed out that the youngest child often feels inferior. Likewise, Adler suggested, the middle child has trouble developing a sense of identity because he or she has no special distinction: The middle child is not the oldest, who once reigned supreme, or the youngest, whose place is never usurped.

Perhaps Adler placed undue importance on the ordinal position of the child and its impact on character and personality, but the majority of U.S. presidents were the oldest child. Because they assumed the highest position in the "national family," we might conjecture that being the oldest child while growing up is good preparation for a later leadership role. Captains of industry, and others who assume leadership positions, have frequently been the first born in their families.

When a child is one of three or more siblings, he or she faces certain advantages and disadvantages. On the positive side, when a child is part of a group of siblings, the child has to learn quickly to cooperate and to consider the needs of others in order to survive peaceably. There will always be competition and jealousy, for no family is exempt from sibling rivalry. But children in larger families, studies show, are more sensitive to the wishes of other siblings and cope better with their jealousy. Sociologists Ernest Burgess and Harvey Locke report that children in families of three or more siblings cooperate better, show less envy of their siblings, and learn early to work in groups.

One of the best examples of how a large family fosters cooperation and limited jealousy among siblings is the Israeli kibbutz. Dr. Bruno Bettelheim has reported that youngsters who live in what amounts to large families become group-minded and cooperative, even willing to die for their country. On the other hand, Bettelheim points out, these youngsters, in contrast to children raised in smaller families, show a constricted range of emotion, limited spontaneity, and certain symptoms, such as bed-wetting, that can be traced back to a lack of individual attention. Bettelheim's studies also seem applicable to our own culture. Regardless of ethnic background or socioeconomic status, children from large families are better team players and more cooperative, but show less emotional spontaneity and fewer signs of anger because their individuality has not been fostered.

Also, children from large families are usually more self-reliant and have more advanced social skills than children from smaller families. The social psychologist Morton Deutsch talks of children from large families possessing better "role repertoires," meaning they adapt more easily to many social situations.

A recent study of high school graduates who took college board examinations showed that children from large families did not achieve as well as children from smaller families. It was inferred that accommodating the needs of many siblings induced anger in children, which interfered with learning.

As we know, a child learns best from a teacher when given love and attention from his parents. There is no doubt that a child from a smaller family has greater opportunity for parental attention. Hence, the learning process is easier for parent and child alike. Educators know that one-to-one tutoring, or a small class, holds many advantages for students of all ages. The children feel important, not lost in a mass of other children, and this feeling motivates them to take in what the teacher offers.

Yet, learning is not directly correlated with family size. If a child is warmly and consistently cared for by the parents, motivation to learn will be high. But, regardless of family size, if what the child has ingested emotionally from his or her early environment is unpalatable, the child's learning capacity may be hindered. Children become able learners when their first teachers, their parents, respond with warmth and care to the children's questions, enjoy their children's curiosity, and give them individual attention.

HOW PARENTS OF LARGE FAMILIES CAN HELP

Even though a family is large, parents can meet their own emotional needs and those of their children, and they can help each child become a person in his or her own right. This requires three main attributes: sensitivity to the child's unique position in the family; an awareness of where the child is in his or her emotional development and a desire to meet the child's emotional needs along the way; and understanding how each child feels toward the siblings and the mother and father.

Parents should try not to show favoritism or to play one child off against the other. In a large family, where the demands on parents are many, there may be a tendency to make one of the children a parental surrogate. Usually this role is assigned to the oldest child. Such an assignment has its advantages and disadvantages for the child, the siblings, and the parents.

Delegate Responsibility—But Not Too Much

On the positive side, the parents are not as harassed when they delegate responsibility. The oldest child feels special and learns to be a leader. The younger children now have the benefit of three parental figures and receive more attention than they usually would.

On the negative side, since the oldest child is often seen by the younger ones as the parents' favorite, the younger siblings may assume that the parents do not hold them in the esteem they do the eldest. There is nothing wrong with giving children special responsibility and tasks commensurate with their age and abilities, unless the large family divides into camps, with the elders on one side—the oldest sibling and parents—and the younger ones on the other. This fosters envy and competition that adds to sibling rivalry and unhappiness.

Parents also must guard against placing too much responsibility on the oldest child. Some parents may abdicate their own responsibilities by informing the oldest that anything that goes wrong with the younger ones is his or her fault and that he or she will be punished when the younger children misbehave. As a result of such pressure, the oldest child may develop deep guilt and a punitive conscience. The child will resent not only the younger siblings, whose misbehavior is heaped on his or her head, but also the parents because of the adults' excessive demands.

It is important for parents to keep in mind that regardless of the ordinal position of a child in the family, each child is first and foremost a unique person with special interests, talents, and characteristics. Oldest children are frequently given too much responsibility and regarded too often as little adults. While parents understandably want to use their oldest child as a helper, they often overlook the fact that the oldest is still a child and often needs help in coping with his or her own life. The child does not exist only to help the younger siblings.

Just as the oldest child is frequently looked on as possessing too many adult qualities, the youngest child is frequently kept an infant far too long. Parents have a tendency to forget that the youngest child wishes to grow and master tasks.

Do Not "Scapegoat"

To make matters worse, the oldest child can be made a scapegoat by the younger siblings. They may continually defy the older brother or sister and refuse to obey and allow him or her to be punished by the parents for not doing the job well. "Scapegoatism" is a frequent problem in a family of three or more. The youngest, as well as the oldest and the middle ones, may be used in this unsavory fashion.

When any group, particularly in a family, has three or more members, there is always the tendency for two to gang up on the third: "Two's company, three's a crowd." Consequently, parents of three children invariably have to cope with two of the children wishing to shut out the third. This kind of exclusion exists in many forms.

Sometimes, parents indirectly foster this form of exclusion. We have seen parents occasionally join in scapegoating; this resolves nothing, but merely perpetuates the hidden anger and resentments. When in any family two children gang up on a third, the parents should ask themselves: What are we doing to foster this?

Two parents consulted a therapist because their youngest son was being scapegoated by his two older sisters. The parents joined with him against their two daughters in the disputes. The therapist learned, after several consultations, that as children both parents had felt like scapegoats in their families. They joined their son in order to continue their old battles with their own siblings. When parents become aware of the hurt and anger they feel from their past, they begin to realize that helping a child fight it out with siblings is a futile battle.

As this boy's parents came to accept their rage at their own siblings, they empathized more with their two daughters. The fights diminished, because the parents had less emotional investment in the perpetuation of the anger. Family battles are fought over and over in future generations if the anger is not understood somewhere along the way. Angry parents create angry children.

Accept Your Own Feelings

When mothers and fathers are willing to accept their own human feelings, whether they are rage, sexual desire, or dependency wishes, the parents are better equipped to cope with the feelings, wishes, and impulses of their children. This is why we constantly talk about the importance of parents facing themselves, exposing to themselves and to each other their own fears, wishes, and past experiences that may have wounded them in some way.

When parents find that advice about child-rearing does not work, it is usually not that the advice is bad but that parents find it difficult to accept the advice. For example, most parents would agree that it is better for a child's questions about sex to be answered. But, if parents feel anxious about their own sexuality, they cannot accept this advice with much conviction. Similarly, when a parent is told that it is necessary to set limits for a child, it is the rare mother or father who disagrees. Yet many parents find it difficult to set firm and appropriate limits because they feel they are being too negative.

When a parent is unable to put into action what he or she knows intellectually is sound child-rearing, the parent should ask: What is it about this advice that upsets me? If the parent cannot set limits, he or she should ask: What aggressive thoughts are stopping me? If the parent cannot discuss sex, he or she should ask: What sexual thoughts of mine are interfering? If the parent cannot resolve a rivalry problem between two siblings, he or she should ask: What rivalry in my own life is asserting itself?

Parents who have three or more children generally find it difficult because they have to say "no" more often, face more demands, and cope with more frustrations. But, when parents genuinely like each other, can share responsibility for the children, and are compassionate and empathic with each other and the children, their tasks are less onerous even though the family is large.

Don't Blame Each Other

Despite the fact that more children may induce more difficulties, the parents' source of harassment often lies not in the children but in the marital relationship. It is helpful for parents to talk over their conflicts with each other without recrimination.

It is almost impossible to rear healthy children and to provide for smooth sibling relations when parents are not emotionally supportive of each other. Good relationships between siblings are an inevitable consequence of a warm relationship between parents. When siblings are fighting and hating each other, some or all of the time, parents should ask each other: How much of the time are we spending fighting—in front of the children or behind their backs?

Problems in a family are never resolved when parents blame each other. As Otto Pollak, a sociologist and family therapist, said, "Family therapy works best when there is shared blame," in other words, when all family members take responsibility for family conflicts. Family therapy, like family life in general, works best where there is shared blame and mutual empathy. When you feel understood, and understand the other person better, your need to blame diminishes.

All human beings have a tendency to blame others rather than to assume responsibility for themselves. Parents blame children and children blame parents and each other for the difficulties of daily life. This is true of husbands and wives, teachers and students, employers and employees, friends, and nations.

We all have a tendency to try to maintain that infantile feeling of omnipotence and perfection. How can we possibly ever be wrong? To blame others and not recognize our own frailties and responsibilities in marital or parent-child battles is really an attempt to maintain these infantile fantasies. When spouses, parents, and children can assume more responsibility for what goes wrong in personal relationships, they move away from the grandiose state of an infant and toward a more mature outlook on life.

Thus, when we find ourselves blaming others, we should ask ourselves: Why do I find it so threatening to accept responsibility for this situation? Many people feel that by assuming responsibility for personal relationships they become vulnerable. Nothing could be further from the psychological truth. The mature person is able to say, I am not perfect. I can be wrong.

A parent does not always have to be right in the eyes of a

child either. A parent who says, I was wrong—I am sorry, will endear himself or herself to the child. If a parent is wrong and can admit it, that means the child is entitled to be wrong once in a while too, and he does not have to strive for absolute perfection.

Respect Each Other, Each Child, and Yourself

Not every large family has to be like a kibbutz, where group-mindedness is fostered and individuality repressed. Many parents are able to give individual attention to three or more children, despite the fact that three often is "a crowd." Siblings will enjoy a large family if the parents show a spirit of enjoyment rather than resentment, and also show respect for each other and for the children.

Respect is a word not used often enough. A relationship of any kind—lover and lover, spouse and spouse, parent and child—is doomed without respect. The sad truth is that we cannot show respect for another if we lack respect for ourselves. Just as charity begins at home, so does respect. It comes from the ability to be honest with oneself, to know the bad as well as the good, the primitive self as well as the civilized self.

Respect comes from the feeling that we are human and possess both hateful and loving feelings. Respect also comes from our capacity to be humane rather than harbor feelings of violence and vengeance. Robert Burns wrote, "Man's inhumanity to man makes countless thousands mourn." We are inhuman when we use violence as a way of coping with another human being. Violence in the world has become a way of coping with unhappiness, and in our country we see an increase in battered wives, in the physical abuse of children, and the destruction of the self through drug addiction, alcoholism, and suicide.

Respect for oneself is often low, because to love is seen as depleting rather than enhancing. One woman in therapy said, "I feel I lose my head when I have a sexual experience with a man I love." She saw love as taking away her power, her sense of reason. Impotent men, and men who suffer from other sexual inhibitions, often feel the same way.

A common reason people become violent and wish for revenge is that they feel powerless, like a small child trying in vain to combat an angry parent. If we carry this attitude into adulthood, we will have to fight hard for self-respect, always in our mind the helpless, angry child.

Children need to grow up seeing respect between their parents and receiving respect from their parents, if they are to feel respect for themselves. We cannot emphasize too strongly the importance of respect as a requisite for a happy child who will grow into a happy adult.

We could say that respect for a child starts when the child first lies in the cradle. Freud believed that the seeds of violence and murder germinate in the nursery, and this is equally true for the opposite emotions of love and trust, which hold in them the quality of respect.

7

SEXUAL CONFLICTS OF SIBLINGS

WHEN SEXUALITY STARTS

Every child has a normal curiosity about his or her body and its functions as well as about the body of the opposite sex. Every child is also curious to find out what goes on behind the closed doors of the parents' bedroom. A young child will want to know where babies come from. A slightly older child may explore the body of the opposite sex, wishing to know the differences. These are natural developments as sensual desires grow stronger, and parents should not be shocked or distressed. Masturbation is also a normal activity. The child who is too frightened to masturbate at one time or another is excessively frightened of his or her sexuality.

Psychoanalysis has made a major contribution to child raising by discovering infantile sexuality. Until the early twentieth century, it was believed that children did not have erotic drives or sexual fantasies. Sexuality was expected to appear suddenly at adolescence.

The idea of a child possessing sexual feelings was sometimes so threatening to adults that a youngster discovered masturbating or even expressing sexual curiosity was admonished or even severely punished. The psychohistorian Lloyd DeMause points out that for centuries children were treated as little adults except when it came to sexuality. His research shows that the expression of any sexual interest by children led to brutal beatings and at times even to murder at the hands of their parents.

Fortunately, today many mothers and fathers are able to acknowledge the fact that every child is intensely interested in his or her body and the pleasurable feelings it can produce. Parents are aware that sensual wishes and fantasies exist at each stage of a child's psychosexual development. Every child receives the first erotic gratification from nursing and suckling. Other sensual feelings follow from urinating and defecating. As early as three years old, children may have fantasies about sexual intercourse. Sometimes they even want to try it if they have slept in their parents' bedroom and seen them in the sexual act. However, a three-year-old's fantasies about intercourse are apt to be distorted. As one little boy said, "A baby is born by Daddy putting his penis in Mommy's peepee hole." He was interpreting the act of sexual intercourse as mutual urination.

But, despite the advances in our thinking about the sexuality of children, there still tends to be a too-narrow perspective on the part of some parents and educators. They often think in terms of a sudden leap from childhood innocence to adult sophistication. But, erogenous zones, such as the mouth, anus, and skin, arouse pleasure in the young child—and continue to do so throughout life.

The wish for sexual gratification has to be reckoned with at all ages. A child is a sexual being at infancy, in grade school, and in high school. However, the degree to which he or she understands or is capable of sexual intimacy is limited at first.

The concept of infantile sexuality was originally met with disbelief when Freud first described it at the turn of the century. But it is now recognized as having profound implications for the capacity to give and receive love, as well as to express oneself sexually. Infantile sexuality also lies at the core of neurotic and other psychological difficulties.

Freud theorized that civilization, generally speaking, was founded on the suppression of instincts, mainly our sexual and aggressive drives. He said: "Over and above the struggle for existence, it is chiefly family feeling, with its erotic roots, which has induced the individuals to make this renunciation." In other words, we give up our early sexual wishes in order to live peacefully within a family.

HELPING SIBLINGS ACCEPT SEXUALITY

Therapists and researchers who work with children can offer much evidence to justify abandoning the notion of the "original sin" of sexuality. Parents often do not give the sexual dimension of a child's life the attention it deserves because they still consider sex basically "sinful."

Sexual feelings play an important part in conflicts that may arise between siblings. There are numerous books and pamphlets that prescribe methods of helping children accept their sexual feelings. But, though providing the facts of sexuality to a child is essential for the child's maturing, there is another important but insufficiently appreciated issue involved in whether or not the child accepts his or her sexual feelings—the quality of the sensual relationship children observe between their parents and with their parents.

Love and sexuality can be only superficially taught from a textbook. A child is more apt to accept his or her own sexuality if the parents enjoy being spontaneously affectionate and tender with each other and with their children. All the technically correct answers in books about sex cannot ward off threatening fantasies of sex as bad and evil if a child lives with parents who constantly fight and torment each other.

When parents quarrel, a child often feels forced to take sides. If the child habitually favors the parent of the same sex, heterosexual development may become stunted. However, if the child usually sides with the parent of the opposite sex he or she will feel extremely guilty and expect retaliation from the rival parent, which can also hinder sexual growth.

The important point is that the parents' sexual conflicts and their distortions of sexual matters inevitably become their children's conflicts and distortions. To avoid this, parents should discuss their sexual feelings with each other. Such frankness will not only provide more gratifying sexual expression for them, but will enhance their children's ability to accept their own sexuality.

Incidentally, when a child does not have two parents who love each other, and does not see love expressed as part of the parental relationship, the child's sexual identity may become disturbed and sexual capacity is apt to diminish. A child needs to witness parents showing warm physical affection as well as experience such affection from both parents. Moderate, continuous, tender contact between parent and child is a must for the child's emotional and sexual development.

Answering Questions About Sex

Though we emphasize the importance of the child witnessing a pleasurable relationship between mother and father as crucial to feeling that sexual desires and thoughts are natural; nonetheless, parents and educators must factually answer a child's questions. But they must remember that the content of the answers is less important than the attitude toward sex that they reveal. If the adult is anxious and embarrassed, the content of the answers will have little effect. The child will believe that sex is anxiety-provoking and embarrassing. As in all educational experiences, the student must feel understood by the teacher. If there is no empathy, learning about sex will be only an intellectual experience for the child that will not appreciably benefit his or her sexual or emotional life.

Sexual desires are powerful in everyone, but they can be tamed and accepted by children if parents accept sex as a genuine fact of life by answering a child's questions when asked, giving the facts appropriate to each stage of a child's development, and recognizing that siblings at different ages need different kinds of information.

Parents should answer questions about sex as they arise. Children need or want very little information at any one time.

Frequently, parents distort the wish of a child to know, feeling obligated to give a three-hour seminar when a child asks, Where do babies come from? All the child probably needs to be told is that a baby grows inside a mother's body. This will satisfy until the child is ready for more information. As a child asks more detailed questions, he or she requires more detailed answers.

Sometimes parents think a little knowledge is a dangerous thing and that the child will use the knowledge in a destructive manner. Only when parents have a distorted notion of sexuality and transmit this distortion to the child will he or she use it destructively. Body parts should be called by their correct names, such as *penis, anus,* and *vagina.* The child should be told exactly what takes place when men and women have sexual intercourse, that a man's penis is placed in the woman's vagina and that this is a mutually pleasurable experience. When conception is described it should include the fact that sperm is deposited in the womb, meets the egg, and causes the baby to grow.

Simple, frank statements are usually not shocking to a child, unless the parent behaves anxiously. It is important for parents to keep in mind the age of the child and to gauge the child's responses. Most children start to show interest in sexual matters at about three or four years old. This is the time they begin to concoct romantic fantasies about the parent of the opposite sex and become interested in the differences between the sexes.

One mother tearfully reported that she was unable to cope with her five-year-old daughter's questions about sex. Though the mother had answered the questions truthfully and in a kindly tone, the daughter insisted she wanted to see how intercourse happened. When her mother told her she would not be allowed to do this, the daughter attacked her mother as mean. The daughter added defiantly that she was going to sneak into her parents' bedroom and watch them have sex. "And when you fall asleep," the daughter said triumphantly, "I'm going to shove you out of bed and be alone with Daddy."

The daughter, like almost every little girl her age, wanted to replace her mother in her father's affection. The therapist helped the mother to understand that when her daughter realized her mother and father both understood the strength of her wish and would not punish her for it, her provocative manner would diminish. Often, children ask questions about sex in such a provocative way because unconsciously they wish to be punished for what they sense is their taboo sexual curiosity and excitement. They feel guilty about both their erotic desires for the parent of the opposite sex and their competitive feelings for the parent of the same sex. As Freud kept telling us, no one motive ever accounts for an intense feeling.

Obviously, a three-year-old asks different sexual questions than a ten-year-old. Parents are often upset when a ten-year-old asks a sexual question in front of a three-year-old sibling. This does not need to be a problem. If the parents are relaxed with their ten-year-old and answer the questions frankly, this easy-going atmosphere encourages both children to relax about their sexual feelings and fantasies (fantasies accompany every feeling we have). Just as a three-year-old loses interest in a discussion of advanced mathematics, the child will lose interest in discussions about sex that are too advanced. Children take in only what they are psychologically ready for.

Even in today's supposedly enlightened atmosphere, many parents have difficulty accepting their sexual feelings toward their children, and accepting their children's sexual feelings toward them. Some parents still think, if I feel a sexual desire it's the same as having sex. As a result, they flee from discussing sexuality with a child or they talk in an impatient, angry or embarrassed way.

Parents psychologically relive their own lives at each stage of a child's development. Therefore, if they grew up in a home where sexual discussions were taboo, they are apt to be inhibited in discussions of sex. Or, out of rebellion toward their parents, they go to the opposite extreme and talk incessantly about sex. The latter propensity may lead to undue sexual stimulation for the child. If a child hears discussions about sex as a steady diet, the child may think that it is the only important feeling in life.

A divorced mother insisted on describing to her twelve-year-old daughter all her flirtations with men, as though to say, men still find me sexy even though your father walked out on me. She was sharing the details of her sexual life with her daughter, which could only be confusing and arouse many conflicting feelings in a twelve-year-old.

As siblings develop, sometimes we see one child more open and spontaneous about sexual feelings than another child who is inhibited and silent. How can this happen in the same home? Earlier, we suggested that parents unwittingly ascribe different parts of themselves to different siblings. The child who openly talks about sexual feelings is displaying one part of a parent's personality while the child who cannot express sexual feelings has taken on the parent's guilt about sex. If parents watch siblings in action, often they can see a mirror image of the two sides of themselves.

SEXUAL PLAY BETWEEN SIBLINGS

Young siblings, before adolescence, often dress and undress in front of each other, share a bedroom or a bathroom. It is a fact of life that when any two children share a room, they are bound to be interested in each other's bodies. If they did not show this interest, they would be abnormal. But parents often cringe when they note their children's sexual interest in each other. To rear siblings in a constructive way, parents need to accept the fact that siblings will indulge in sexual play and experimentation. This is part of normal sexual development.

A normal child will want to play doctor with his or her siblings, enjoy playing house, and occasionally want to wrestle so he can feel his sibling's body close. When parents notice such sex play, they should accept, as the siblings do, that the children are learning about their own sexual feelings in a playful manner. We are convinced that if more parents would acknowledge to themselves and their children that a certain amount of sexual experimentation is enjoyable, we would see far fewer unhappy children and, in turn, far fewer unhappy adults.

When parents accept the idea that experimentation is enjoyable, they are in effect giving permission to their children to accept that sexual gratification is not an act to be abhorred but to be explored. As parents encourage their children to experiment with roles, for example, giving them a chemistry set so they can become acquainted with scientific exploration or a

Monopoly game to interest them in business, so they should acknowledge to their children that sex play is an age-old, universal act. This will help the children to accept, rather than reject, a key dimension of their human condition.

It is crucial for parents to make sexuality a legitimate and indispensable part of human functioning. Much of the self-hatred in children and adults stems from their hatred of sexual wishes as "evil." So many children and adults find it difficult to like themselves because they were castigated when they masturbated or explored the bodies of children of the opposite sex. Had their parents acknowledged that sex play was a normal part of growing up, the self-esteem of these children would be much higher.

Unfortunately, too many parents believe that if they do not prohibit sexual experimentation in their children, they will have wild sexual animals on their hands who will become perverts. If sexual play is excessive or compulsive, to the exclusion of other interests, it is probably because a child is unconsciously pleading with the parents to discuss his or her sexual conflicts. Any excessive action on the part of a child is usually a disguised cry for help. The child either feels fearful, angry, and guilty because he or she is driven by intense sexual feelings, or the child is not receiving enough attention from the parents, or both.

WHEN SIBLINGS DENY SEXUAL FEELINGS

Often, when siblings keep a distance from each other or constantly fight, they are acting to deny their normal sexual feelings toward one another. The inhibited sibling, as well as the openly angry one, is usually the child who has not been helped to accept sexuality or the sibling's sexual feelings.

Troubled parents brought for therapy their seven-year-old son and five-year-old daughter, who engaged in bitter fights and angry name-calling. As the therapist studied the situation carefully, it dawned on him that these two youngsters were trying to live out fantasies of marrying each other. He wondered whether this brother and sister naturally wanted the same relationship they saw their mother and father quietly enjoying and thought that the siblings might be fighting with each other as a protection against sexual feelings—a denial of their fantasy of marrying each other.

The therapist suggested to the parents that they talk to both children in a family conference, which the parents agreed to do. The father opened the conference by pointing out that he remembered when he was a boy that he often engaged in fights and name-calling with his sister. The mother, as planned with the father beforehand, then recalled she had fought one-upmanship battles with her brother. Both children smiled when their parents pointed out that they, as children, had engaged in the same acts their own children were involved in. The father then asked the children, Can you guess why brothers and sisters fight so much?

There was a long, embarrassed silence on the part of the children. Then they looked at each other and began to giggle, as did the mother and father. The mother asked, "How come we're all giggling when we're talking about fighting?" Again, a long, embarrassed silence ensued. Then the son ventured the opinion, "Maybe there's something funny about fighting." His sister added, "We always end up laughing after we fight." To this the father said, "Did you know that when people like each other, they laugh with each other?" Both children then agreed, and the daughter observed, speaking to the father, "You and Mommy laugh a lot with each other and you like each other."

The father then said to the son and daughter, "Mommy and I think that when you fight, you'd really like to be married to each other, like we are." The family conference again erupted into laughter. They were acknowledging that the fighting between brother and sister was really a modified form of sexual play.

One of the most successful ways parents can make sexuality, or any human experience, acceptable to their children is to acknowledge that when they were children they experienced the same wishes, the same anxieties, and the same conflicts their children experience. Children feel reassured when they hear that their parents held the same fantasies they possess. If parents can permit themselves to admit their childhood experiences to their children, they keep the children's guilt at a minimum, reduce anxiety in their youngsters, and nurture self-esteem. All the children above needed for harmony was permission from their parents to enjoy their fantasy of marrying, about which they had felt so guilty that they had to deny it in anger and fighting.

In another instance, two brothers, eleven and eight years old, were constantly at battle in somewhat violent wrestling matches. The parents were understandably concerned that the boys would harm each other and tried to stop the fighting. The parents consulted a therapist, who believed that though the home was essentially happy, the two brothers needed their parents' permission to love each other. The wrestling matches were a defense against expressing love. Through the wrestling they could feel close bodily contact, maintain a macho image, and deny all sexual feelings.

The therapist suggested to the parents that they tell their sons it was natural to want to feel close to each other, and the brothers' need to wrestle vanished. They began to share other, less violent interests, the older brother taught the younger one to play baseball and the younger brother helped the older one find new stamps for his collection.

Parents need to understand that sexual attraction between siblings becomes a problem only when parents are not sufficiently loving and empathic with their children. Such parents are likely to keep sexual topics out of the conversation most of the time, as though sex were obscene. When siblings engage in frequent, overt sexuality rather than occasional play and experimentation, it is usually because they experience strong yearnings for an understanding of their feelings, yearnings their parents have ignored.

A thirty-five-year-old single woman had difficulty sustaining a relationship with one man and went for therapy. Though she was extremely attractive, she said, "I have always felt ugly and unwanted." Reluctantly, with shame, she confessed that between the ages of eleven and fifteen, she had engaged in incest with an older brother who had seduced her and that she had felt ashamed ever since. In her relationships with men, she unconsciously fantasized each one as her older brother and felt such guilt that she soon had to break off the relationship. Her guilt had made her feel ugly.

She also revealed that her father was a cold, detached man who never appreciated her femininity or beauty and who criticized her as dressing like a bag lady. He was afraid of his sexual feelings for her, and his son had acted out his father's repressed desire with his sister. This woman had committed incest with her brother to express anger at her demeaning father. As she began to realize how angry she had been at him for not loving her as she thought a father should, she could forgive herself for the act of incest. Though we may feel alarmed at reports of incest between brothers and sisters, such sexuality generally is the sibling's way of finding the love lacking from a parent.

THE OEDIPAL CONFLICT IN SIBLINGS

Siblings sometimes act out the Oedipal conflict with each other instead of with the parent. Often when siblings, particularly of the same sex, become excessively competitive, they are displacing their competition with the parent of the same sex. A twelve-year-old, ferocious in his tirades against his fifteen-year-old brother, was helped to realize that he was transferring his angry feelings toward his father. As he came to understand his natural competitiveness with his father during the Oedipal stage, he lost his need to tear down his brother. It is only by becoming aware of a feeling that we can cope with it.

The sibling relationship offers a rich interaction with the Oedipal dilemma. Starting in the pre-Oedipal period, before the age of four or five, the sibling relationship already sets up the first triangular relationship—between the child, a sibling, and a parent. This prepares the child for the second triangle, which occurs at the Oedipal stage, involving the child, the mother, and the father.

The pre-Oedipal relationship with a sibling offers a child a chance to develop ways of coping with conflicts over jealousy, love, and hate. However, this period differs from the later

Oedipal period, when the child not only has to contend with conflicts centered around the relationship with the parents, but also with conflicts over the parents' relationship to each other. The child's fantasies and defenses against and responses to parental authority become enmeshed with ambivalence, rivalry, and envy.

Some of the same issues are dealt with in both the pre-Oedipal and Oedipal phases, but the pre-Oedipal modes of coping affect the way in which the child confronts Oedipal issues. The child who experiences intense rivalry with, and envy of, a sibling in the pre-Oedipal period, is more prone to intense conflict over the same feelings in the Oedipal phase.

If, as sometimes occurs, a three- or four-year-old in the pre-Oedipal stage is the victim of violent physical or sexual abuse by a sibling, parent, or other adult, the child will find it very difficult to proceed psychologically to the Oedipal stage. The child may remain forever a victim of the crippling experience and live a child's sexual and emotional life—one of masturbation or abstinence because of terror.

During the Oedipal period, the sibling relationship offers the child an opportunity to repeat many features of his or her relationship with the parents. One sibling, by sublimation in fantasy and play, may substitute for the coveted parent. The sibling may be more malleable than the parent in a child's efforts to resolve the Oedipal conflict. Where there is a large age gap between siblings, an older sibling is apt to be a good substitute parent, offering chances for resolving the Oedipal conflict in ways that are constructive. For example, the love of an older sibling may enable a younger sibling to keep his or her sexuality alive through the latency stage after a severe Oedipal disappointment. Or, a younger sibling can serve as a substitute baby for an older sibling's ardent wish to have a baby with a parent and give some gratification as the sibling takes on the temporary role of a protective parent.

THE SIBLING RELATIONSHIP AND CHOICE OF SPOUSE

The sibling relationship is usually a factor in the choice of a marital partner because that choice involves overcoming the incest barrier against the peer generation, which derives from the sibling relationship.

Dr. S.M. Abend, a psychoanalyst, in his article "Sibling Love and Object Choice," written in 1978, described two cases involving siblings whose preference in love partners as adults was influenced by an unconscious attachment to a sibling who had been exhibitionistic and seductive in childhood. The later choices were made on the basis of resemblances to siblings rather than to the opposite-sex parents.

Another noted psychoanalyst, Dr. Samuel Ritvo, believes that though the family life of siblings prepares them in many ways for marriage and the establishment of a new family, "the unconscious revival and repetition in the marital relationship of intense conflicts [from childhood] may be the bases of marital problems."

A thirty-year-old woman, unable to settle down and marry, came for treatment, complaining, "Why do I always fall in love with men who are five or six years younger? Then I feel guilty and have to break off the relationship. I feel I am seducing them." During therapy, she spoke of adoring her brother, five years younger, as she grew up. She mentioned casually how she hated the woman he married because she considered him her property. The therapist helped her to understand that her attraction to younger men was a repetition of her love for her brother. Because of her incestuous feelings she could accept no one man. By the time she left therapy she had fallen in love with a man five years older and looked forward to marrying him.

INCEST BETWEEN SIBLINGS

Parents may unconsciously encourage incest between their children. A parent who, as a child, had intense sexual desires for and fantasies about an older sibling may unwittingly push his or her child toward sexual fantasies, even sexual acts, with a sibling.

A man told his therapist, "My wife and I have virtually no sex because we have a brother-sister relationship." He had displaced his forbidden incestuous feelings from his sibling to his wife.

Sexuality among siblings in their early years can be thought of as a response to both stimulating and inhibiting influences on the part of their parents. In the very early sibling relationship, an infant is not yet an immediate source of pleasure to the older child. Love for the younger sibling comes gradually, at first stimulated by the fear of losing the parents' love if hate is shown to the newcomer, then out of identification with the parents' attitude toward the infant, and finally in response to the infant's admiration of the older sibling. This sets the stage for the older child to come to terms with rivalry and jealousy. Eventually, through the influence of his or her conscience and the sublimation of angry, violent feelings, hatred evolves into a nurturing, protective, and loyal relationship to the younger sibling, if all goes well emotionally.

Siblings eventually offer one another excitement and pleasure via their mutual sexual play, with rapid shifts from one erogenous zone to another. Siblings, if they are not too frightened, may become, for a while, sexual objects for one another. If they do not eventually find other interests however, they may negatively influence each other's sexual and personality development.

There can be destructive influences in acting out sexually with siblings. A younger sibling may be forced to submit to the curiosity and sexual aggression of an older sibling, lacking the strength to protest. This premature stimulation of the younger sibling's sexual responses will either hasten sexual maturation or throw the child into regression.

What can parents do to avoid sibling incest? They can do their best to enjoy each other sexually and emotionally. While this may be a tall order, it is perhaps the major factor in discouraging sibling incest. When parents are unhappy with each other, this unhappiness affects their children in many ways. If a mother or father feels frustrated in the marriage, there is an unconscious tendency to use the children in a subtle, yet real, sexual manner. Many a father uses his daughter in a clinging, seductive way because he is not enjoying his relationship with his wife. The same is true of the mother who feels resentment and lack of warmth toward her husband. She will tend to use her son or daughter as a sexual substitute, getting undressed in front of the child or hugging or cuddling excessively and in the end overstimulating the child.

When children are sexually overstimulated they tend to turn toward each other for sexual gratification. When sibling incest occurs, it may be because the parents are not enjoying themselves sexually or emotionally, and are living vicariously through their children's sexual behavior. They may unconciously promote this behavior by giving a brother and sister the same bedroom and tacitly approving of the siblings' getting dressed and undressed in front of each other, or bathing together. While bedroom arrangements and bathing arrangements can be rationalized and justified, family therapists have found time and again that when there is an excessive amount of sexual play between siblings, the parents are somehow encouraging this, frequently not realizing their role in the situation.

One of the first questions parents should ask themselves when they see excessive sexual play between their children is, How much of this sexual play am I subtly encouraging? When parents discover in what manner and why they are encouraging this excessive play, they should then ask, Why am I discouraging myself from sexual relations with my spouse but encouraging the children instead? The answer frequently involves an honest discussion between the parents, perhaps with a therapist.

Just as sexual play occurs between brother and sister, it can also occur between brother and brother and sister and sister. Often, sex play between siblings of the same sex is a way of getting ready for sex with the opposite gender. A certain amount of sex play between siblings or friends of the same gender is quite normal. We should expect it in every growing child. But when the sex play is constant, the chances are that the children are finding heterosexuality a dangerous thought and an act to be avoided.

Parents often ask, What do we do when we discover our children engaged in sex play? It is important, though difficult, for a parent to respond with understanding in this situation. But it is reassuring to the parent to know the children may have unconsciously arranged to be discovered and thus are subtly asking to be controlled. Parents sometimes forget that when children engage in overt, unsanctioned behavior the chances are that the children are asking that limits be set. Thus, in a warm but firm manner parents should confront children in sexual play saying: I'm going to have to stop you, even though I know this may be enjoyable. Such a statement in no way condemns sexuality but suggests that there is a time and place for sexuality to be gratified.

SUBTLE PARENTAL SEDUCTION

Sometimes a parent will unconciously practice subtle seductions on a child. A father or mother will kiss a child passionately on the lips, or allow the child to sleep in the same bed, or parade nude in front of the child. Such subtle seductions affect many more children than actual incestuous attacks. It would help children if parents became aware of the subtle seductive behavior in which they engage and which may harm a child. There is a narrow line between consistent love and tenderness, and an overseductiveness that may affect a child's emotional and sexual development.

Overseductiveness may be expressed by excessive kissing or embracing, which creates guilt in the child and envy in the siblings. Overseductiveness may also be less obvious. For instance, the parent's denial of sexual feelings for the child may be so strong that the parent is wary of even touching the child tenderly. A thirty-year-old woman just completing three years of therapy said, "Now I understand why my mother always seemed to hate to touch me. I thought of her as the frozen woman. I realize she was so afraid of her sexuality that she could not even bear the touch." Another denial of sexual feelings is the use of violence by the parent to express acute fear of the erotic touch.

Every parent is seductive to some degree, since sexual feelings are always present in everyone. We may feel sensual toward a member of the opposite sex, a member of the same sex, a child, a mother, a father, a sister, a brother. What we do with our sexual feelings depends on how strongly we are driven by them.

When a child receives premature sensual stimulation by being allowed to sleep between the parents in their bed or frequently seeing them nude, this may seem like added attention and preferential treatment over the other siblings. But it also induces overexcitement, adds guilt and shame, and may harm the child's psychosexual development.

It is, of course, excessive seduction of a child if a parent allows the child to witness the act of sexual intercourse. A woman of twenty-seven, unable to marry, recalled that when she was a little girl her parents would leave their bedroom door open at night and sometimes she would peer across the hall into her parents' room early in the morning and see them engaged in sex. She told her therapist, "I remember feeling both frightened and fascinated." She started having sex with numerous boys in high school, became even more promiscuous in college, and then went into therapy to find out why she had not been able to marry.

The sexual intimacy her parents had invited her to observe by leaving their door open constituted an early sexual arousal she was later unable to control. Just as a child should not be pushed to learn beyond his or her ability to assimilate knowledge, so the child should not be subjected to a sexual scene beyond his or her ability to understand. Children interpret the act of sex as a violent one, believing the father is beating the mother. The parental act of sexual intercourse belongs between husband and wife, and a child should not be made a third party to the physical act of love.

Though our society has always taken a strong position against incest, it also acknowledges that no parent is exempt from sexual fantasies about his or her children. Perhaps there has been an incest taboo because of these fantasies, since society has recognized that when parents and children live together for years there is bound to be sexual excitement toward each other. But, as we have pointed out, when parents are sexually and emotionally gratified with each other, the chances of using their children as sexual objects are slim.

But, when a father or mother sleeps in the same bed with a child there is inevitably a disturbed relationship, particularly a disturbed sexual relationship, between the parents. One of the most damaging acts a parent can perform is to promote sleeping arrangements between children and parents. This should always be avoided, because it fosters excessive stimulation in the children and deep guilt response to the incestuous feelings.

Subtle ways of seducing children occur by dressing or undressing in front of them, taking showers and baths with them, or permitting too easy access to the parental bedroom. When such acts take place children do not feel normal, they are bombarded by incestuous fantasies, have to deal with much masturbatory guilt, and in general lose respect for themselves. When parents find themselves permitting the children easy access to their bedroom they have to ask, Why are we arranging to be interrupted in whatever we choose to do by our children? Do we want to involve them emotionally in the act?

Once again, for siblings to grow into mature adults who enjoy the sexual dimension of their lives, they need to have their sexuality appreciated by their parents. This means that the parents will neither condemn sexual expression by the growing child who is starting to be aware of erotic desires, nor will the parents be overseductive to the child, in either a subtle or an overt manner.

8

SPECIAL KINDS
OF SIBLINGS

All siblings are unique and have their own idiosyncrasies. However, there are special kinds of siblings who may exert a deep influence on the rest of the family and be unduly influenced themselves, in either beneficial or destructive ways, by their siblings.

THE ADOPTED SIBLING

The adopted child represents only two percent of siblings. Most writers and commentators on the subject of the adopted child refer to adoption as inevitably a painful, sometimes traumatic, experience for everyone involved. Particularly in our culture, adoption usually occurs when something has gone wrong in the lives of both the natural and adoptive parents. The natural parents usually are unwilling or unable to care for the child they have conceived, or the adoptive parents have been unable to conceive a child themselves.

Regardless of the circumstances, relinquishing a child is always painful for parent and child alike. From the point of view of the adoptive parents, the decision to adopt a child often occurs after years of pain and disappointing attempts to conceive a child. We have rarely seen adoptive parents who did not feel a personal sense of failure. Regardless of how many times the child is told that the adoptive parents are his "real" parents who chose him above other children, he almost never feels quite at home. As one adopted child said wistfully, "My real parents gave me up." The adopted child tends to feel abandoned and sad.

It is a difficult task for every child, adopted or not, to learn to get along with parents. Children, as we have noted, are quick to distrust their parents' motives and often exaggerate their reactions to parents' anger or discipline. But the adopted child has an additional burden the natural child does not face. The adopted child not only has to cope with the normal angry feelings children have toward parents, wondering do they really love me? Do they really want me? But the adopted child must face the fact of being born to one set of parents and being raised by another. This is confusing to a child who cannot yet, perhaps never, understand why his natural parents have forsaken him.

Adoption will always pose special hazards for the child's emotional development. Virtually every research report on adoption suggests that adoptive children become patients in psychotherapy more often than nonadopted children. This not only shows the extra emotional burden the adopted child bears, but also suggests how difficult it is for many parents to cope with the adopted child. However, we also feel that adoptive parents tend to be responsible parents on the whole, and are more likely than natural parents to take the adopted child and his or her siblings for therapy.

In the majority of studies on adopted children in therapy, common symptoms include behavior characterized as aggressive, anti-social, provocative, or impulsive—in other words, they lack control of their violent impulses. But in spite of the many difficulties adoption entails, most research shows that it is the optimal solution to the problem of the unwanted child. Studies report that the adopted child functions better and feels more at ease than the child growing up in an institution or temporary foster home.

The Special Problem of Adoption

The adopted child and his or her parents and siblings have a number of special problems. One reason is the change in care-takers during early infancy, which may not provide the consistent love and tenderness a newborn needs to develop what Erikson calls inner certainty and trust. While Anna Freud and other authorities on the emotional development of children have advocated that adoption procedures take place as quickly as possible, legal and societal constraints often prevent this necessary speed. Adoptions are rarely finalized in the first few months of a baby's life, and many adoptive parents, knowing this, cannot truly give of themselves on a spontaneous basis. Particularly during the first few months of adoption, parents often feel like workers hired for a job but not assured that they will keep it. This is obviously a situation that induces great anxiety in the adoptive parents and in the baby.

About ten percent of adoptive parents later produce children of their own. Ironically, when wives and husbands stop trying so hard to be biological parents they are often better able to conceive a child. The drama between siblings intensifies when one child is adopted and one or more are biological. Though it is commonly believed that parents tend to favor their biological child over the adopted child, this is not always true. When parents doubt their ability to bring up a child and are uncertain about their self-image, they may view a child born to someone else as superior to their own. They may feel that their own child is defective in some way, as they feel defective. Certain adopted children feel superior to their siblings because the parents believe them to be superior. But, if parents view the adopted child as not quite belonging to the family, this sense of exclusion may cause the child to feel unwanted. If an adopted child is to flourish emotionally, the adoptive parents should allow themselves to feel that the child is as much theirs as a biological child would be.

One question adoptive parents often ask is: When do you tell the child he is adopted? Rarely is the answer simple. Just as sexual information is acquired by children when they are ready to accept it, so a child's questions about adoption are answered by the behavior and attitudes of the parents. The child will sense when the parents want him or her to know.

And just as sexual questions should be answered directly, so should questions about adoption. Most professionals agree that because adopted children so frequently experience knowledge about their adoption as a blow to self-esteem, it is probably better to withhold information until children are five or six years old. At that age, the child feels more secure about his or her place in the family. It is at that age also that a child starts to ask questions about sex and reproduction, showing a greater interest in bodily sensations.

Even when parents are giving and mature, most children, when told they are adopted, initially feel there is something wrong with them. Dr. Herbert Wider in his article "On Being Told of Adoption," published in the *Psychoanalytic Quarterly* (1977), points out that all adopted children with whom he worked "held the distorted belief that their biological mother had cast them out to die and they were found by the adoptive mother."

This is a fairly common fantasy. Freud spoke of the "family romance" each child imagines, based on the feeling, I don't like my family, I will find another family that will treat me royally. Just as most children imagine they will find a mother and father who are far more loving than their own, and that their natural parents are imposters, the adoptive child wonders: Who will really love me? Where will I find the family that is truly mine?

Thus, it is important for parents to remember that all children, whether biological or adopted, feel cheated at times. One way they cope with this imagined deprivation is to fantasize gaining a new set of parents who are more lovable and more loving. Probably every child at one time or another dreams of running away from home and finding a good mother and father. This is a more intense, complicated feeling in the case of the adopted child who is uncertain as to who his or her parents actually are.

As Siblings—Adopted and Natural—
Grow Up

Just as all sibling relationships range between feelings of love and hatred, with some siblings loving each other more than other siblings, the relationship between the adopted and the biological child shows a broad range. It is important for parents to consider the unique aspects of this particular sibling relationship.

When parents think of the adopted child as better than their natural child, the siblings will mirror this view in their reactions and interactions. A young adopted boy, Norman, was referred to therapy because of his selfish, contemptuous attitude and destructive behavior toward his sister. The therapist worked with him on his need to dominate and denigrate his quiet sister, born to the parents three years after they adopted Norman. The therapist learned that Norman echoed the views of his self-doubting adoptive parents, who considered themselves inferior to his natural parents. They kept telling him he was very special, unusually brilliant, and far superior to his sister—a reflection of their fantasy of him. Not only did the therapist help Norman accept the reality that he was a member of the human race—no easy task for many of us—but he worked with the parents to modify their view of Norman's natural parents.

Some of Norman's smug attitudes also related to his own doubts about his lovableness and intelligence. This was a factor in his belligerent behavior toward his sister, a defensive attitude reinforced by the parents. When the therapist interviewed Norman's sister, she said in an understanding way, "He thinks he's so smart just because he's adopted," as though to excuse his overbearing attitude.

Many times, a biological child who fantasizes that his or her real parents live elsewhere, also believes that the adopted sibling has found the ideal parents that the natural child has only fantasized about finding. This occurs particularly when parents favor the adopted child and the natural child feels like an outcast.

There is a tendency on the part of some parents, as we have pointed out, to favor the adopted child. This attitude is sometimes understandable, tinged with the feeling, sometimes conscious, sometimes unconscious, that the parent has "saved" the child by giving him or her love and a home. But such an attitude does not help either the adopted or the natural child: The adoptive child becomes suspicious of the parents' overzealousness, and the natural child resents it.

It is difficult for parents not to make comparisons between the natural and the adopted child. But, as we have suggested throughout this book, when a parent finds himself making comparisons between his children, he is having difficulty dealing with parts of himself that he dislikes. He is projecting onto one child all the characteristics and attitudes he does not want to face in himself. That child can be the adopted one, as the parent says to himself, "These unlikable qualities belong to the outsider." Or it can be the natural child as the parent accuses his spouse of giving the child "bad genes." A mother and father were concerned because their eight-year-old adopted daughter was defiant and rebellious, whereas their natural child was respectful and always well-behaved. The parents found themselves protecting their natural child against the onslaughts of the adopted child. In time, these parents came to understand that they were projecting aggressive, hostile fantasies onto the adopted daughter, making her the family scapegoat, and intensifying the natural rivalry between the two children.

Whether the natural child comes first or second, if parents note tension between the two children, they should ask themselves, as any parent of two or more natural children should, "What am I getting out of this, emotionally speaking?" And also ask, "What am I contributing toward this tension?"

When parents have one or more natural children they should ask themselves why they feel the need to adopt another child. The reasons, like the reasons for having children in general, vary. They range from a desperate attempt to solve the parents' own conflicts to the healthy wish to take part in the wholesome growth of children. Sometimes parents feel their only child needs a companion. And sometimes, as their only child becomes more independent, the parents need a child who will depend on them exclusively.

Regardless of the motives for adopting a child when parents

already have children, the adopted child sooner or later feels either special or inferior. Either way, there will be tension between the adopted and the biological children. For the tension to be resolved, it must be understood by the parents, especially their part in creating it.

It is often very reassuring for parents, particularly adoptive parents, to realize that all children and all parents, at one time or another, feel ambivalent. And that all siblings, regardless of whether they are natural or adoptive, will feel ambivalent. As Dr. Harold Blum, a psychoanalyst, points out in his article "Adopted Parents" in *The Psychoanalytic Study of the Child* (1983): "Adoptive children can be just as much loved and lovable as natural children; and in families where there are both natural and adoptive children it is not necessarily the natural child who is favored. Parental love can certainly be gratified in the rearing of an adopted or a natural child, and this love, as well as the mature qualities that all parents can bring to their parenting, means that adoptive parents can be the full equivalent of natural parents."

WHEN THERE ARE TWINS

The Specialness of Twins

The idea of twins connotes great specialness. Parents are considered to be special, Herculean creatures, when they produce twins, and twins are considered special beings. But little has been written about the many problems twins induce in parents and in each other.

Though we have always felt a strong compassion toward all parents, we feel even greater compassion for the parents of twins. There is always work for the parents who bear twins: their duties rarely let up. It is a big task to feed, diaper, and put to sleep just one infant, but it is vastly more difficult when a twin is also screaming for attention. Then, after the screaming twin is also fed, diapered, and hopefully put to sleep, the parent sighs with relief and begins to relax, only to hear the first twin crying again out of some need. Because our society considers twins special, and thinks the parents of twins should be overjoyed, not overtaxed, the parents often deny their own distress. Our message to them: You have the right to feel burdened.

Because two helpless, demanding babies are such a burden, it is inevitable that from time to time the parents may wish that they had only one child. This is a completely natural feeling. A man, married a year, said in a tone of desperation to his therapist, "My wife and I have just learned she is going to give birth to twins. We expected only one child. We have only one room to set aside. What are we going to do?" He confessed, "I'm excited but I'm also angry. Part of me feels like murdering one of the twins. I kept having the thought one of them might die in childbirth. I feel so guilty at such a hostile wish, I haven't even been able to tell my wife about it." He added, with an ironic laugh, "I wonder if she feels the same way." This ambivalence is probably shared by every parent who ever faced the idea of twins. But, by admitting to his thoughts, this man was better able to deal with the birth of his twins, for then he would not repress his anger and guilt.

Because the parents of twins carry such a burden, one of the most serious problems that twins have to confront is that they rarely receive sufficient individual attention. Society, as well as parents, tends to view twins as a symbiotic pair—two persons merged as one. It is the rare twin, particularly when an infant, who knows what it is to be alone or to be treated as a single individual. Some parents assume, as the mother of one set of twins put it, "They can take care of each other." They may often have to, but it is not the same as parental care—it is a love tinged with rivalry.

Twins often feel they do not have a right to their own possessions, their own feelings, or their own time with a parent. This is compounded by parents and a society who believe that twins think the same way and should be dressed the same way, and that they have an empathy for each other that makes up for the lack of empathy in harried parents. One reason twins frequently develop such closeness is because they feel the parents do not give them enough attention.

Sibling rivalry between twins is often strong because each twin does not feel he or she has a special place in the parents' heart or home; they feel merely part of a twosome. Yet, because twins so often feel compelled to be a symbiotic pair, they may squelch their rivalrous feelings and their wishes for independence, and deny their individuality. Parents of twins often feel uncomfortable when their children fight it out. A mother of twins said, "If I see two other children fighting I don't get as upset as when I see my twins fighting because I look on the twins as a unit, not two persons. I start to think of one of my twins as committing suicide when they attack each other."

The Closeness of Twins

In the process of growing up, many children, especially when there is only one child in the family, develop imaginary playmates. Such a playmate, like a friendly sibling, helps the child feel more loved, emotionally more secure, and is there to offer solace when the child feels disappointed or frustrated. In fact, many children wish to have a twin. The relationship to the imaginary twin represents a partnership never threatened with separation. The psychoanalyst Dorothy Burlingham pointed out that children can often overcome a feeling of deep loneliness by having an imaginary twin. She compares this to a child's real or imagined possession of an animal as a companion. (It is interesting to note that Burlingham, the youngest of the four daughters of artist Lewis Comfort Tiffany, had twin sisters born just before her.)

Anyone who has worked therapeutically with twins knows that as much as children yearn for closeness and companionship, twins possess it perhaps too intensely. When therapists treat a twin, whether child or adult, a common problem appears: Twins feel they do not have the right to their own belongings, attitudes, and feelings. Said one man in his late twenties, a twin suffering from acute depression, "Every time I do my own thing, I feel like a murderer." Anything he undertook apart from his brother made him feel he was obliterating his twin.

He consulted a therapist when he intended to choose a profession different from that of his brother, a college professor. The client wanted to study economics and perhaps be a stockbroker, but he felt that to try to differ from his brother was disloyal, as though he were splitting from his twin, and casting him off. As he began to accept the fact that he was a person in his own right and entitled to separate emotionally and professionally from his twin, he felt free to plan his career in his chosen field of economics. He also felt freer in other ways, such as not compulsively visiting his brother every week.

Many a twin feels as though he or she is murdering the other twin by trying to be separate emotionally, because twins consider themselves what Burlingham called *à deux*—an inseparable twosome. Everyone has always responded to them as a unit, and their desire for individual attention and praise is usually frustrated so frequently that their anger is intense. As we know, every angry feeling carries with it the unconscious wish to murder the instigator of the anger.

In the relationship of one twin to the other, there exists many of the same problems as between any two siblings. Twins also compete for attention from their parents. There is usually a tendency for one twin to be active, the other passive. Often the activity or the passivity is constitutional, and parents have to allow for these individual differences in the aggressive drive.

While all siblings identify with and copy each other, twins have a tendency to engage even more in such activities. It is difficult for parents to allow twins to identify with each other and yet to help them become emotionally separate and to achieve self-identity and independence. This becomes even harder when they are identical rather than fraternal twins.

It is helpful for parents of twins to recognize that, whether twins are fraternal or identical, each has different feeding patterns, different strengths, and different liabilities, and to respect these differences. One of the ways parents can encourage the healthy emotional development of twins is to recognize that they are separate individuals who do better if each possesses his or her own clothes, own room, own special abilities, and own place in life.

There is a tendency on the part of some parents to unconsciously arrange for one child to be good and the other bad, and this can also happen with twins. There are families where one twin turns out to be Dr. Jekyll and the other Mr. Hyde. In one such family, twin sons were born to a father, an editor of a leading magazine, and his wife, a staff writer on the magazine until she resigned to give birth to and bring up the twins. Mark, born first, proved easy to care for, a smiling and quiet baby, but John, born second, started to wail the moment he saw daylight and never seemed to stop. A friend told the mother, listening to John cry each time she visited, "That child is going to need special care—or be in therapy for years."

As the twins grew up, John kept expressing his unhappiness in moodiness and discontent while Mark had a smiling, sunny disposition. Both were bright students, and at twenty-one, Mark took a job at a publishing house after graduation from college, but John did not know what he wanted to do. He still lived with his parents, and he started to take drugs and to drink heavily. He would lose his temper when he got drunk, and once his parents had to bail him out of jail when he got into a fight with a stranger at a bar.

At this point, his mother took John to a therapist. After several sessions with members of the family, including the twin brother, the therapist suggested to the parents, "I think you made John into the good child, Mark into the bad one, over the years."

The mother said angrily, "John was a little devil! From the moment he was born, he never gave me any peace. Mark was an angel. He's always been my helping hand in controlling his angry brother."

As the therapist worked with John, he thought that the second baby to arrive had needed special care, perhaps had suffered physically as he was born, emerging after Mark. Whatever the cause, he showed his pain first by crying and later by his moodiness. He became a burden. Undoubtedly, his parents unconsciously conveyed to him that he was a nuisance and that his depression and complaining angered the rest of the family. For example, the therapist noted that the mother smiled at Mark each time he walked into the room for a family session, whereas she frowned each time John entered, as though expecting only despair and anger from him. One time she told the therapist, almost in a whisper, "I think there are moments I hate that boy."

Slowly, the therapist helped John to face his feelings, to express his rage at his mother, father, and twin brother—whom he considered both a best friend and the rival he wanted out of the way. As John became more aware of his repressed fury, he gave up the drugs and alcohol. After two years of therapy he took a job with a Wall Street firm, intending to become a broker, and he moved to his own apartment, finally breaking away from his parents and his twin.

The Effect on a Non-twin Sibling

Being a sibling of twins is a difficult emotional task, and several analysts have written on the subject. Burlingham noted in her book *Twins*, "The fuss and excitement over the twins not only by the mother but by everybody who comes into contact with them can only increase the jealousy of the older non-twin sibling." This of course also applies to a younger non-twin sibling.

All children, as we have said, react to the birth of a sibling with various degrees of jealousy and hostility, but when two babies arrive at once a sibling's reactions are intensified. The child feels utterly displaced from the love of parents who now have to give extra time and care to two newborns. Moreover, for many parents, having produced twins brings such gratification that they spend much time in adulation and awe of them. In such an emotional climate, the single sibling will feel abandoned, helpless, and enraged.

Whether the twins precede or follow the birth of a lone sibling, the sibling faces a difficult time and needs special attention. It is necessary for parents to understand the single sibling's rage and envy, and to give attention to these feelings so that he or she will not feel like a complete outsider.

THE ONLY CHILD

Studies show that the only child is rarely free of the fantasy that a brother or sister may be born any day. The child is usually confused because he or she does not welcome a rival, but on the other hand would like to have a brother or sister as a playmate and companion.

Thus, the child lives with the wish that the parents produce another child, but also with the fear that if they do, the only child's reign will collapse and he or she will be banished. As a man, now forty-two, an only child, told his therapist, "When I was a boy I envied my friend next door who had an older brother and a younger sister whom he could talk to all the time and play with. But deep in my heart I was frightened to death my parents might produce another child I would hate for taking my place as the star."

With only children, it is the amount of emotional support a child receives from the parents that either destroys or promotes his or her sense of well-being. Sometimes, only children have what psychoanalysts term an overdeveloped superego: They feel they must be very moral, very obedient, and always do the right thing. One of the main reasons for this behavior is their guilt at having aggressive thoughts toward their parents. It is difficult for them to be aware of or to express hostility because they feel they have been given so much. As one only child asked, "How can I show dislike toward my parents when I have received everything I want from them?"

Parents of a lone child often find it difficult to be the target of anger from their "one and only." Yet, to help the child grow up happily, it is necessary for parents of all children—the only child, twins, siblings of many different ages—to feel the freedom to experience, and frequently to express, the whole range of human emotions—the pleasurable and the painful, the "good" and the "bad."

Though this book is about siblings, it is important to keep in mind what happens to a child who does not have siblings. While most only children frequently hunger for a brother or sister to help them cope with the loneliness and aggressive wishes they feel toward the parents, one of the major difficulties is that the only child finds it hard to share. Obviously, when there has been no sibling to share attention or tangible objects such as toys, food, and television sets, there is a tendency for only children to feel entitled to have all their demands gratified pronto, without having to consider others' needs.

The only child, because he or she has the exclusive attention of the parents, frequently finds it difficult to withstand frustration and take no for an answer. Elementary school teachers are often able to pick out the only children in the classroom because they demand attention more often than the others and find it difficult to remain silent when they are ignored. They strive hard to be the teacher's pet, trying to recapitulate the situation at home where they are the center of attention.

The narcissism of an only child tends to be high, for in many ways the universal wish to which Freud referred, to be "His Majesty, the Prince," is fulfilled. In living with an only child, parents have to be careful to avoid indulgence, but it is not easy to do so, because so much of the parents' life energy is invested in the child. When parents have only one child and the child is angry, sad, or rebellious it is more difficult for the parents to cope, than when there are other children a parent can turn to one and feel loved. With an only child, parents need to support each other much more to make sure they are in strong agreement about limits, prohibitions, and permissions. While all children need two parents who enjoy each other and who work together on their children's behalf, the only child needs this even more. If the only child feels that the parents are united against him or her, the anxiety becomes powerful, the guilt heavy, and self-hatred inevitable.

9

THE LOSSES AND MOURNING OF SIBLINGS

THE GREAT LOSS

The most devastating loss a child can suffer is the loss of a parent through death. When a parent, even if harsh and brutal, is snatched away by death, a child mourns deeply. Nothing is more disruptive to a child's life. And, according to psychologists Stephen Bank and Michael Kahn in *The Sibling Bond*, the death of a sibling is a close second. These psychologists point out that, while each child experiences the death of a parent or a sibling in a unique way, no child is exempt from feelings of devastation.

Let us look at how children experience the idea of death. The very young child, has no concept of what being dead means. When the child reaches three or four years of age, he or she begins to discover death when a pet dies or an elderly relative disappears forever. Usually, there is little or no concern about death until a child is five or six years old. While the age varies from child to child, it seems clear that it takes time for a child to comprehend the full meaning of death.

A girl of three, whose father died in an automobile accident, when she saw his body at the funeral home, said to a friend, "My daddy went to sleep for a while." This was her fantasy of death. A five-year-old boy who watched the burial of his father, who died after a severe heart attack, informed his mother, "Daddy's gone on a trip." A six-year-old, informed that her mother had died from pneumonia, said, "You mean she's going to spend a little time in heaven with God and the angels before she comes back."

A more realistic attitude in a child occurred when a father took his five-year-old daughter to the aquarium for a Sunday afternoon's outing. They passed a huge tank of tropical fish in which an angelfish lay inert at the bottom. The little girl stared at the dead fish in horror. Her father explained gently, "The fish won't hurt you. It's dead." "Is that what dead is?" she asked. The father told her reassuringly, "It was a very old fish. It lived a long, happy life, swimming around peacefully for years."

The little girl shuddered and said, "Let's get out of here," as though death were more than she could bear. Her father realized that this was her first experience with death. She had suddenly become aware that if animals could die, so could she and her parents and siblings.

The death of a loved one brings forth fantasies about death, including the death we have wished to inflict on those toward whom we have felt hatred. We cannot escape our fantasies any more than we can escape breathing. Dr. Martin Grotjahn, a psychoanalyst, has written eloquently of the nature and power of fantasy in childhood:

The greatest mental dread of a child: that he may someday lose control of his bad thoughts, and they may suddenly get loose like a swarm of bats from a cave after sunset. We live in constant dread that our unconscious may find its way to consciousness and may overwhelm our controls, then Mr. Hyde would overpower Dr. Jekyll and would do all the bad things we had hoped were safely repressed a long time ago.

Many a youngster feels: If I ever let myself go, I will destroy everyone who has ever hurt me. I will kill my mother and father, brothers and sisters. We are all afraid of the monster within—our unbridled, primitive passions, which include the desire for revenge.

Though a number of psychologists attribute the young child's inability to understand death to a lack of sufficient intellectual capacity at that stage of life, we believe it is the need in the child to deny the reality that he or she will never again see the person. This thought is simply too terrifying to the child.

The defense mechanism of denial is often used by an adult to hide painful feelings as he or she refuses to accept the reality of a loved one as dead. An eighty-year-old man, lying in a hospital after a slight stroke, kept calling for his mother who had died nineteen years before, wanting her to comfort him. Parents who lose children sometimes cannot accept the losses and they continue to talk to their children as though they were present. Like children who make believe that an absent one is present, these parents react with the same defense—denial. If adults find it painful to accept reality of the death of a loved one, surely a child, far more vulnerable and far less resourceful, will feel all the more need to deny death.

Despite the fact that children do not acknowledge death easily, many of our famous folk tales for children involve death. In both *Little Red Riding Hood* and *Jack in the Beanstalk* the threat of death comes from devouring. Since young children are preoccupied with the mouth and with eating, it should not surprise us that death through cannibalism is a popular theme at this age. However, in fairy tales denial reaches its ultimate— death can be conquered. The victim may return to life, as Little Red Riding Hood is rescued intact from the wolf's stomach after he has eaten her.

Perhaps because the idea of death is so overwhelming, a child will begin to believe strongly in an afterlife. The dead person has disappeared from sight but continues to remain alive. A seven-year-old boy in therapy said, "Nobody will ever die—not my mother, not my father, not I." He made the remark at the time his grandmother was near death. He was obviously protesting the idea of death meaning gone forever.

How well or poorly a child copes with the death of a parent will depend to a large extent on how free the child has been with his or her aggressive impulses. If the child has been taught to suppress anger and never speak of resentments, then the death of a loved one may be disastrous. In a child's mind, thought is equivalent to the deed. The child who lives in a repressive atmosphere believes a violent wish to be the same as an act, and tries to conceal the wish but resents controlling his or her rage. Thus, the child harbors secret, guilt-producing fantasies of wishing the mother, father, or sibling dead at times. Should this catastrophe actually occur, the child is convinced he or she is responsible because of such a wish.

For several years, a therapist worked with a forty-year-old woman who deprived herself not only of sex, but virtually all pleasures. One day she related a memory of a traumatic moment when she was 10. Her father had slapped her across the face when she defied his order to clean up her room and she had thought in fury, "I hope he drops dead!" When he died of cancer a year later, she was convinced her wish had killed him. She was gripped by intense guilt over the thought that she was her father's murderer and therefore never entitled to any pleasure. She had to be punished for her foul deed.

In his brilliant paper, "Mourning and Melancholia," Freud referred to two reactions to death. When there is only a limited amount of unexpressed hatred toward the one who dies, sadness and mourning will follow but little guilt and agitation. The mourner is able to move on to others for love and gratification. But, when there is intense, undischarged, unconscious hatred of and anger toward the dead person, the survivor believes he or she is guilty of murder and remains forever guilty.

When a parent dies, all children need the chance to go through the three stages of the mourning process: protest, despair, and detachment. This conclusion evolved from the observations of small children by the psychiatrist Dr. John Bowlby of the Tavistock Child Developmental Research Unit in London, famed for its psychological studies of children.

But, all too often, children are afraid to show their protest and despair, so they never reach the detachment stage where they can start to replace the lost person. It is important, in helping children cope with death, for parents to help the children verbalize their feelings of protest and sadness and acknowledge a legitimate anger because the dead person is no longer available to love and be loved. If a parent sees a child depressed for months after the death of a parent or other family member, the parent can be sure the child is punishing himself or herself because the child believes he or she has caused the death.

Parents have to guard against reenforcing the child's tendency to deny the reality of death by saying that the deceased has just gone away for a while or is sleeping and will return, or by ignoring all mention of the death. In this case, the child's bereavement and anger go mentally underground and may affect the child's schoolwork, play, and personal relationships.

A child may use the mechanism of denial for a long time, even years, and appear unaffected by the death. This takes place with adults too; it is often called being in shock. After any crisis, there is a tendency to deny reality. But parents should not be lulled into thinking a child is unaffected by a relative's death because the child behaves as if nothing has happened. In this case, denial is inevitably taking place, and it is helpful for the parent to make comments acknowledging that it is difficult to accept that the dead person is no longer there. It is easier to pretend the dead person is still there, or expected to return, but it is healthier for the child to face the reality in as nonthreatening a way as possible.

When there is more than one child in a family, siblings often help each other mourn if given permission to do so by a parent. A friend's children were helpful to each other during the deaths of their grandparents. While it was painful for the parents to observe their sons crying, they appreciated what the children did for each other to relieve their mutual suffering.

When a parent feels ambivalent toward the deceased, it is often difficult to help the children overcome their distress. Before helping the children, the parent may have to discuss his or her own ambivalent feelings with another adult to become fully aware of them. The task of helping the children must eventually be tackled; otherwise they may remain depressed for a long time.

Parents today are generally well prepared to answer their children's questions about birth and sex, but they may be troubled when they have to deal with questions about death. Parents can be most helpful if they acknowledge the reality that someone they loved has died and explain precisely how the death occurred—through illness, accident or suicide. The parent should help the child verbalize anger, sadness, and helplessness and verbalize these feelings for the child if he or she cannot do this alone.

WHEN A SIBLING DIES

Almost comparable to the loss of a parent, is the loss of a sibling. The loss is acute and difficult for a child to handle because no child is exempt from resentment toward a sibling. A child will always hold envious and rivalrous feelings for a sibling, wishing the sibling were out of the way, then feeling guilty. If a sibling dies, the other children feel responsible for the death because of their hostile fantasies.

A nine-year-old boy had a younger brother who died of leukemia. While at first the boy seemed to show no feelings of grief, after a few months his schoolwork and his relationships with friends deteriorated. He would play games in which he pretended he was dying—as though stepping into his brother's shoes.

Both children and adults often say, I'd rather it were me, when a loved one dies. The boy's therapist helped him get in touch with a very painful fact—that part of him, like all siblings from time to time, wanted his sibling dead. This was not easy for the small client to hear and to accept. For a long time he protested against the idea, but when he finally accepted this thought and began to feel his anger and verbalize it, he felt less depressed and functioned better in school and with friends.

This was only part of the task, however. He also had to accept that he missed his sibling and that his younger brother, though hated at times, was also a good friend. The therapist did in therapy what parents can do at home with youngsters who have lost a brother or sister—help them accept their anger and grief.

Many parents have a tendency to idealize the dead sibling and find it difficult to accept resentments and disappointments in the remaining children. This happens because the parents deny their own resentments and disappointments in the deceased child. Usually when a child dies he or she has been ill for a long time and the parents have shown excessive attention and concern. The remaining children, also understandably, resent this and are in a way relieved when the ill sibling disappears forever. But their guilt is then strong. The survivors may need to be convinced that their anger did not destroy the sibling.

Even after death, the influence of the sibling lives on. It is important for parents to let their children reminisce about the lost sibling, keeping in mind that there are always pleasant and unpleasant memories and that both need airing. There is a deep tendency in all of us to idealize the dead. We repress our anger, righteous or not, at the time of someone's death because we feel on some level that if we acknowledge it, we are the killer. Perhaps the most traumatic death of all occurs when the sibling commits suicide. The surviving sibling thinks: What did I do to make my brother or sister want to take his or her life?

The rate of suicide among adolescents has risen drastically in this country. There are now six times more adolescent suicides than twenty-five years ago. Every ninety minutes a teenager commits suicide—6,000 died at their own hands last year, and there were 400,000 attempts. Even younger children are taking their lives. Recently, an eleven-year-old boy killed himself after writing a school essay about a homesick youngster's suicide. The child was reportedly having difficulty making friends in the new town to which his parents had moved.

Teenagers who had seriously thought of killing themselves appeared on a recent television program to tell how tormented they felt. An eighteen-year-old boy said, "I felt so unable to cope with my own expectations and what the world expects of me I thought I might as well take my life." Another reported, "I wanted to say, 'Mom and Dad, when I feel this sad, this bad, I need you to take the time to listen to how I feel and hear me out.' "

Others spoke of feelings of inadequacy, of going nowhere,

unable to reach out to anyone, of helplessness and hopelessness. As one put it, "I can't go on anymore. I feel unable to carry out what my parents expect." He added, "Every parent wants the perfect child. Because the parent wasn't perfect. I feel like asking my mother and father, 'How do you expect me to be perfect. You weren't.'" Once again, this unattainable ideal of perfection crops up as the root of so much unhappiness in childhood and adulthood.

A parent's guilt over the suicide of a child may be overwhelming. The parent feels at fault, a failure. A mother whose fifteen-year-old son shot himself when his girlfriend jilted him said sadly, "I didn't pay attention to the signs he gave out." She listed them: "He didn't seem to care about anything; he just lay listlessly on his bed for hours. He gave away some of his prized possessions to friends. He told one friend, 'I've been thinking about killing myself.' His friend said, 'Don't talk like that—don't be crazy.' My son then thought he was psychotic, and it made him more depressed. I thought it would all pass. It didn't."

One of the most difficult deaths to face is that of a twin. Inasmuch as twins tend to be identified as one unit, there is a tendency for a twin to feel the loss acutely, as though a part of the self is destroyed.

Because twins are so often seen together, eat together, sleep together, frequently are in the same classroom, and dress similarly, the loss is powerful and can never be minimized. Because twins are invariably looked upon as a pair, there is bound to be a certain amount of resentment in each. Whenever a twin is in therapy, the therapist knows that sooner or later he will hear, "I never have my own space. I never live my own life." Consequently, there is a hidden resentment in all twins toward each other, at times verging on death wishes. When a child wants his or her twin out of the way and the twin actually dies, this is cause for a great deal of guilt, since the live twin feels a murderous wish has come true.

Therefore, the death of a twin is so traumatic because rarely is there such closeness between two people so early in life and a closeness mixed with so much resentment. When these two feelings work together, as they do with twins, the death of one twin is usually responded to with melancholia and intense self-accusation.

The parents' task in dealing with the loss of a twin is also very difficult, and usually parents are so deep in mourning themselves that they feel unable to help the remaining twin. They have to permit themselves to feel their agony for a while and not strain to become oversolicitous to the living twin, because the latter will sense the lack of sincerity and spontaneity. Parents should acknowledge their own grief and remorse to the remaining twin, and this in itself signifies to the child that it is all right to also feel grief and remorse.

Parents also have to help the lone twin deal with the fact that every brother or sister in the world, particularly a twin, sometimes wants to get rid of a sibling and that the parents felt it themselves when they were children. They need to discuss with the twin the difference between the wish and the deed, emphasizing that wishing doesn't make it so. Because parents are in such a difficult situation themselves at this time it is hard for them to talk about loss and death wishes; therefore, therapy may be a good idea.

THE "REPLACEMENT" CHILD

When a child dies, frequently the parents want a replacement. This is easily understood, for the birth of another child soon after is in many ways helpful in relieving the depression of the bereaved parents. But when a child is replaced, parents have to be very sensitive and understanding as they deal with the new child, and not make unreal demands that the child cannot possibly fulfill.

One boy was told when he was four years old that he was born a year after a brother died. Knowing this, in and of itself, was not too upsetting. His distress was caused by the fact his parents kept mentioning, as though it were a virtue, how similar he was to his dead brother in appearance, thoughts, and acts. This imposed on him the responsibility to be someone other than himself in order to ensure his parents' love. His sense of identity became split between himself and his dead brother, who was idolized after death by the parents. Parents have a tendency to forget the faults of a deceased child and remember only the virtues, perhaps even imagined virtues.

Children, as well as adults, in order to like themselves and enjoy life, have to feel they can be themselves, not a reincarnation of someone else. A rival sibling who died would threaten them severely. Parents should not name the replacement child after the dead child.

Parents should permit themselves enough time to mourn the death of a child before they seek a replacement so that they place no extra burden on the new child, and do not ask him or her to make up for the death of the other child. It usually takes a minimum of a year to go through what analysts call grief work. When feelings of helplessness, anger, and grief are discharged over time, the parents are in a better position to greet a newcomer with less conflict, and the newcomer will be far happier.

A word should be said about helping the sibling who has to cope with a replacement child. The birth of any sibling is difficult for a child. Every child thinks: If my parents really loved me, they would not need another child. This feeling can be strong when a child who has shared parents with a sibling who suddenly died finds that a replacement child is shortly expected.

The surviving child needs special preparation, and should be encouraged to talk about the feelings involved in once again becoming dethroned by a rival. This child should also be helped to verbalize his or her mixed emotions about the dead sibling. This is a difficult task for parents as they deal with their revived feelings of mourning for the dead child, the conflicts of the existing child, and their feelings about the expected baby.

When parents can be honest with each other about what they feel, they are in a much better position to help a child accept a new arrival after the death of the sibling.

ILLNESS IN A SIBLING

A common experience of many siblings is coping with the illness of a sister or brother. Depending on the severity of the illness, the healthy child usually has difficulties at this time.

When either a child or an adult falls ill, he or she regresses, wants, and frequently gets, extra attention, and is the recipient of a tender, loving care. Sociologists refer to this as a "sick role."

Dealing with a seriously sick child is a difficult task for parents because not only do they have to administer extra tender, loving care, but they must also recognize that if illness is indulged it can become a way of life, a tempting path to lasting affection. It is helpful for ill children when parents, after providing sufficient rest, medicine, and kindness, start to talk about some of the child's responsibilities, such as resuming homework, regaining physical strength, and seeing friends again. Timing is crucial, for no child or adult wants to hear about responsibilities when downed by a fever of 102 degrees. Everyone, when sick, needs doses of love, but we also have to help children recognize that remaining a patient is not the best way to ensure love.

When illness is severe, as when a sibling suffers from polio or cerebral palsy or is brain-injured, many issues have to be faced by parents. The handicapped child needs extra help in coping with life, but there is a tendency on the part of many parents to go to one of two extremes. Either they deny the child's handicap and try to make the child function as if there were no illness, or they deny the child's strengths and treat the child like a helpless baby. Neither extreme is helpful to the sick child, the siblings, or the parents.

A sick or handicapped child needs special attention but his illness should neither be indulged nor disregarded. Because siblings are frequently rivalrous, we have seen the healthy sibling wish to be sick and the sick sibling wish to be healthy. When parents are confronted with this attitude, they can help both children if they accept that each child wants to be more like the other. This acknowledgment in itself helps both children accept their respective realities with more ease. Honesty is the best approach.

One problem parents face when a sibling is visibly handicapped or very ill is that the healthy brother or sister will feel neglected and angry at the relative lack of attention. In retaliation the healthy child may not even acknowledge to friends the existence of a physically handicapped sibling. This is particularly true when the sick sibling has a permanent, visible handicap. Parents should encourage the healthy child to express his or her feelings for the handicapped sibling, or to express his anger and his shame at having a handicapped sibling. Parents also need to explain to the healthy child that the sibling's handicap is a fact of life that has to be faced by both siblings and accepted by both.

When parents have one child who is ill and another who is healthy, they must realize they cannot ignore the healthy child's problems. Healthy children, as we have suggested, sometimes feel jealous of the attention the ill child draws and it is not uncommon to see a physically healthy child whose sibling is ill feign illness. Parents should consider that the healthy child resents the sibling's illness and may be trying to emulate the sibling to get attention. Often, when parents talk to the healthy child about the idea that illness seems a way of getting love, the child feels better understood and the illness will disappear.

Because there is always competition between siblings, well or ill, when a healthy child notes that a sibling is sick and in a weakened condition, he or she may feel a certain triumph, lording it over the vanquished opponent. But few, if any, children or adults can feel pure joy over such a hostile triumph. Inevitably, there will be guilt, and consequently, when parents see a healthy child appearing morose as a sibling lies incapacitated, the sadness may not be purely sympathy, but may also be a form of self-inflicted punishment over hostile wishes. Often it is helpful for the parents to simply tell the healthy child that they sympathize.

Parents need time for themselves away from all their children. If they do not take this time, whether the children are young or adolescent, the parents will resent them. There are parents who, for various reasons, give too much time to their children and not enough to themselves. Much like the people who overextend themselves at work, such parents do not feel entitled to their own pleasures away from their children. Often these are parents who will feel the inevitable resentment all parents feel towards children from time to time and they have to compensate for their guilt by showing oversolicitousness and overconcern for their children.

When children, regardless of age, emotional development, or state of health realize that parents have a life of their own, though the children may sometimes resent it, they are in a much better position to strengthen their own individuality.

OTHER LOSSES IN LIFE

While no loss is more devastating than the death of a parent or sibling, children face other losses that cause pain. They are the normal, natural losses that occur in the life of every child.

Every step of growth carries with it some sense of loss. The first sense of loss for each child is felt as he or she starts to detach emotionally and physically from the mother. The child goes through another loss when weaned and again when toilet-trained. These first losses may be long out of consciousness, but they live on and affect behavior if they are mourned.

Certain normal losses should occur at specific times in a child's growth, because with each loss comes a move toward independence. For example, if a mother does not wean a child until two years of age, she makes it difficult for the child to separate emotionally from her. If she weans the child too early, when he or she is not yet ready, the child feels a deep sense of loss.

In a general sense, life's first large loss is the loss of trust in the parent. Since a child's world revolves around the parents' every move, the parents become either protectors to be trusted, or people who endanger the child through neglect, people not to be trusted.

Other losses in a child's life include the death of a pet, on whom the child undoubtedly has bestowed love and care; the loss of friends when families move from one area to another because of a parent's change in jobs; and the loss of self-esteem that comes from failing in school, at either studies or athletics. There is also a loss of pride when anything lessens confidence in the self—from a sarcastic remark by a supposed friend to a gaffe that makes a child socially inadequate.

Whatever the loss, parents can help prevent a child from being engulfed in grief by providing other interests, by showing affection, by understanding the loss, and by allowing the child to express sadness.

A child feels a great loss—the loss of love—when a parent speaks sharply or punishes severely. If parents know this, they are less likely to cause such a loss, knowing it is among the most hurtful losses of childhood. This is probably the loss that occurs most often, since the average family does not often suffer early deaths but frequently suffers the voices of parents raised against children who disobey or in some other way offend.

For siblings, as for the only child, the wish to restore what they have lost, or have given up against their will, goes on all their lives. The process of restitution is a continuous one. If restitution is not somehow sought and partially attained, depression sets in as mourning remains unfulfilled. A loss will automatically cause a child to try to substitute another love for the lost one. Thus, loss plays an important part in emotional development and leads to growth if a child can complete the mourning process. This means getting in touch with anger, grief, and guilt.

Sometimes parents are not successful in helping a child face loss. One boy, six years old when his father was killed in an automobile accident, showed no sign of sorrow. He did not shed a tear at the funeral.

His mother was worried at this lack of emotion and took him to a therapist. At the boy's third session, when the therapist asked how he felt about the death of his father, the boy broke down and cried in anguish, at last able to face his deep loss with a sympathetic stranger. He had known how much his mother suffered and hadn't wanted to add to it. He was also afraid to express his own devastating feelings, as though this made him a weakling.

Siblings can often help each other accept losses, especially when one sibling is several years older than the other. Siblings can also console each other in times of loss when parents fail to do so.

THE REWARDS OF LOSS

Out of loss may come not only grief, anger, and a sense of deprivation, but rewards as well. Parents can help children overcome losses by providing a means of restitution and by understanding that the mourning process, when fulfilled, becomes a way to emotional growth.

Some psychotherapists believe that creativity is connected with the early loss of an important person, usually the mother or father.

It is important for parents to understand the powerful role loss plays to a child, not only traumatic death, but sometimes unnoticed losses. The breaking of a treasured toy or the sudden moving away from the community of a close friend may temporarily cripple the child's sense of identity, and prevent the child from achieving in school or being creative. The ability to create, whether it is designing a dress or writing a poem adds immeasurably to self-esteem.

A child who feels deserted when a parent leaves the home may seek restitution for the loss by transferring his or her love and feelings of loss to a pet. One three-year-old boy patted his puppy on the head and said, "You miss your Mommy, don't you?"

Dr. Gregory Rochlin, a psychoanalyst, in *Griefs and Discontents: The Forces of Change,* refers to what he calls the loss complex. During the early years, the fear of loss, the dread of abandonment, and the thought of dying constitute "our three major conflicts," he says. Each conflict acts "in concert with the others as the loss complex."

These conflicts, he adds, are based on three convictions: relationships are tentative, that is, not permanent; stability is threatened by change from within and outside the self; and there exists a deep and necessary dependence on others. Thus losses—and griefs and small mournings—are part of childhood, as well as accompanying the natural traumas of our psychosexual development, such as weaning and toilet-training. Parents, knowing this, can help their children cope with life's inevitable losses, both the large and the small painful ones, so the children can move on to the rewards that lie in restitution.

As parents are able to do this, they make life happier for each child and enhance the relationships between siblings. The more at ease siblings feel about their losses, the more at ease they are with other siblings, and the more at ease they will all be within themselves.

Anxiety is contagious, particularly among siblings, who look to each other for clues to proper behavior. This is true especially of the younger sibling, who depends on the older one as a model. If the older one mourns, the younger one mourns. If the older one is able to handle grief and seek restitution and thus grow stronger emotionally, the younger one is also more likely to do so.

In spite of the many losses endured during childhood, the early years are filled with hope and expectations of pleasure in the fulfillment of realistic dreams. Siblings can help each other, and parents can help their children, to realize those dreams by accepting both the natural losses and the unexpected losses that take place in all families.

In the next chapter, we will examine in detail a specific loss many of today's children experience: the loss of a parent through divorce.

10

HOW SPLITS IN THE FAMILY AFFECT SIBLINGS

A PARENT'S MEANING TO A CHILD

Let us first try to understand what a parent means to a child. We can say with absolute certainty that for a child to mature happily he or she needs two parents who respect, trust, and love each other; who live and work cooperatively; and who, for the most part, stand together as they praise the child, set limits for the child, and plan for the future.

Though we live at a time when two-parent families are becoming less common, all the research on child development, child-rearing, and child therapy points unequivocally to the fact that when a child sees his parents loving each other, the child invariably loves himself or herself and is more likely to enjoy the opposite sex.

If a child is reared by one parent alone, there are bound to be difficulties. Nature abhors a vacuum, and the single parent tends to use the child as a spouse substitute. Any child who has only one parent tends to have adult responsibilities placed on him or her and frequently cannot feel the freedom to be a spontaneous child. In addition, when one parent has to function as two, it is inevitable that he or she feels overburdened and resentful. Thus, the child who lives with one parent is often the target of irritability, anger, and depression.

How can a single parent combat the tendency to make a child a surrogate partner? Though the tendency will always be there, if the single parent wants to provide the most wholesome atmosphere possible for the child, the parent should make sure he or she has several adult interests and relationships. This, to some extent, lessens the pressure on the child. It is helpful for a child to note that the single parent has relationships with adults of the opposite sex. This provides reassurance to the child and makes the child feel less responsible for the single parent's welfare. And, if the child can be present from time-to-time at meals where the single parent enjoys the company of a member of the opposite sex, this also offers feelings of security to the child. If the parent's friend can form a special relationship with the child—taking the child to museums or the movies—this will help even more to assure the child that he or she may remain a child, enjoy childhood, and not be responsible for the parent's happiness.

Another problem that emerges in almost every child who lives in a one-parent family is that the child feels guilty about possessing one parent. Often, the child has a fantasy that the wish to possess the lone parent has resulted in the elimination of the absent partner. The normal wish to get rid of the parent of the opposite sex is magnified a thousandfold when that parent has vanished. The guilt may be overwhelming to a child.

A psychologist was treating an eight-year-old boy who lived alone with his mother, who had divorced his father when the boy was five. At first the boy felt guilt-ridden, as his play with the psychologist indicated. He felt responsible for his father leaving home, and believed he was not entitled to a happy life because he was such a villain.

When the mother made plans for her and the boy to move

from New York to Chicago, where her sister lived, the boy fell into a depression more severe than the one that caused him to enter treatment. He was feeling guilt at "killing off" his male therapist in much the same manner he believed he had caused his father's disappearance.

When the therapist helped him to realize that thoughts don't kill, he was able to feel more self-confident and more entitled to his own wishes and fantasies.

It is a universal belief on the part of children in one-parent families that they have "killed" the absent parent. They may need help recognizing that they are not as omnipotent as they fantasize. Children believe in magic and think they are responsible for the way their worlds are ordered. If a mother or father disappears from the scene, the child automatically feels like a culprit. If the parent understands this and in turn shares this understanding with the child, the latter will feel far less guilty. If a parent has full grasp of the reality of the situation, the child is never too young to accept at least part of it.

In the one-parent family children also seek to create the absent parent in fantasy. They tend to imagine relationships with figures they need. Fatherless children imagine they have fathers and carry on conversations with these fathers as if they were present. Motherless children do the same thing, imagining that a mother is by their side. Every child, at one time or another, has an imaginary play companion who often serves the purpose of a loving, protective sibling. When a parent observes a child spending a great deal of time alone and not taking part in activities with other children, the chances are that the child is engaged in a fantasy.

A divorced woman who had no children had a sister, the mother of two children, who divorced her husband. The husband remarried, and the sister was horrified when her ten-year-old nephew lovingly said to her one day, "Now you are my father."

"What do you mean?" She felt confused.

"Well, you and my mother are very close and since Daddy has gone, I think of you as my father," he said admiringly.

She told her therapist, "I guess any port in a storm for children, when it comes to vanished fathers."

Children need two parents. This is such a strong need they

will somehow find a substitute, no matter what the sex.

Even when children live alone with one parent of the same sex, they can feel guilty because they believe they are the recipients of privileges and pleasures that rightly belong to powerful adults. This explains a phenomenon that puzzles many parents—that is, a child creating a father or mother in fantasy who is a very punishing figure. By making the fantasy parent so punitive, the child atones for the guilt feelings he or she harbors for having special adult privileges and for supplanting the missing parent.

Very often, when children live alone with one parent they feel guilty about the arrangements in which they find themselves. Many a boy starts to feel he is being treated like the superman father he always wanted to be and thought his father was. Many a girl feels guilty, as she lives alone with a father, when she takes over the traditional wifely role, at least in fantasy.

In his paper "The Dread of Abandonment" (1961) in *The Psychoanalytic Study of the Child*, Dr. Rochlin points out that every child left by one parent inevitably experiences this as abandonment. The parent's leaving produces what Rochlin calls a narcissistic injury or a hurt self-esteem, as the child devalues himself or herself and feels: If I were lovable and worthwhile, my parent would not have left me. Dr. Rochlin also points out that abandonment evokes frustration, anger, and even hatred. Since few children can tolerate hatred toward a parent, they punish themselves for the feeling, turning the anger inward.

HOW SIBLINGS COPE WITH ONE-PARENT FAMILIES

When more than one child lives in a one-parent family some of the reactions to the loss of a parent are different than in a family that has only one child. Frequently, a sibling will use a brother or sister as a substitute for the vanished father or mother. A young boy may relate to his older brother as if the latter were his father. The same occurs if the older sibling is a sister.

She can be made into a father, just as a brother can be made into a mother.

On the other hand, it is important for an only parent to recognize that what may appear as sibling rivalry could actually be the younger child competing with the older sibling as if the latter were a restrictive parent. Moreover, when an older sibling views himself or herself as a parental figure the sibling is often more punitive and restrictive to the younger sibling than a parent would be. Why? For one reason, the older sibling savors the fantasized status, for every child wants to be an adult. In addition, the older sibling knows full well that he or she is not a parent and feels uncomfortable about the feigned status. To compensate for this insecurity, the sibling works overtime to be more punitive than a parent would be.

Thus, a younger sibling in a one-parent family may be in a difficult spot. The child not only feels guilty for, in fantasy, causing the disappearance of the other parent, but also feels abandoned. The child wants the love of the absent parent in spite of his or her ambivalence. In addition, the child has to cope with normal sibling rivalry with the older sibling, compounded because the older sibling seems to possess a parental status.

This situation makes life difficult for the one-parent family with two or more children. It requires much vigilance on the part of the parent not to make the oldest sibling a substitute for the missing spouse. The temptation is great, but no child really wants this fantasy fulfilled, it entails too much responsibility and produces too much guilt.

The parent also has much to cope with when dealing with the youngest child, who is apt to feel forlorn and abandoned by the absent parent. The younger child is more defenseless than the older sibling and needs two parents more. The parent who heads the household needs to show the younger child that he or she understands how the child may feel discriminated against by the older siblings, whom the child envies even while fantasizing one of them as the missing parent.

Many men and women who rear children by themselves feel they have to be supermen or superwomen. They deny the human need for reliance on others and find it difficult to accept the fact that their job is often overwhelming. Such parents need to give themselves permission to acknowledge the inevitable resentments and disappointments that being a single parent inevitably evokes.

If a single parent feels he or she has to be perfect, the parent sets a tone for the children, who then believe they do not have the right to feel frustration, imperfections, disappointments, or resentments. All children and parents, to be fairly happy, need to know that because life and people are never perfect, they are entitled to feel angry and frustrated at times. This holds particularly true for parents and children of a one-parent family, where disillusionment may run high.

Just as siblings can be allies as well as enemies, it is possible for siblings in a one-parent family to help each other and to live and work together in harmony. This is more apt to take place when the single parent does not turn one sibling into a spouse substitute, but views the children as children and allows them to develop into adults at their natural pace.

Often, divorced parents unconsciously use their children to try to work out unresolved resentments toward the divorced spouse. When a parent criticizes the divorced or separated mate, this does not help the child resolve the conflicts that follow the breakup of parents. The child then feels obliged to take sides, which causes guilt because of his or her hostility toward one parent.

When a parent criticizes the divorced or separated spouse, the parent fails to realize that the children will resent the critic more than the parent demeaned. Children want fair play between their parents, because they need them both. Thus, it is helpful to siblings living with a divorced or separated parent to hear from time to time that both parents caused the divorce, that both contributed to the marital fracas. How seldom we hear this from divorced parents. But it is always true. Children benefit from the truth and need their parents to tell them the truth. When the truth is denied or ignored, the child resorts to fantasy, distorts the truth, and displaces the magnified conflicts onto siblings and parents in a way that is destructive to everyone.

It is important that parents exclude children from their ongoing battles. An unfortunate byproduct of divorce is that spouses, even when they remarry, often seem all too ready to continue their fights, sometimes for decades. When ex-spouses want to keep up the psychic war, it is easy to use the children as messengers to transmit provocative and hostile messages. A seven-year-old boy in therapy, whose parents divorced and remarried, brings to his father, everytime he visits, some angry message from his mother, such as, Tell your father he's not spending enough time with you. His father then asks him to take back an attack on his mother, such as, Tell your mother she's spending too much money on your clothes.

In one session the boy wistfully asked his therapist, "Why can't my mother and father love me instead of using me as a messenger? That's not my job."

CUSTODY ARRANGEMENTS

Whether a sibling should live with a mother or father, especially when the sibling's gender is taken into consideration, has been a matter of concern to both families and professionals who try to help them.

One interesting suggestion was made in a column by Nadine Brozan, writing about "Relationships" in *The New York Times* on April 21, 1986. She cited the example of a couple divorced when their son was seven, who agreed the mother should have custody and the father would spend one evening a week and every other weekend with the son. But, upon the son's arrival at adolescence, mother and son found themselves fighting much of the time. The father proposed a solution that, according to Ms. Brozan, is "increasingly being tried by the divorced parents of teenage sons." He asked his son, "Why don't you come to live with me?" His son replied he thought this "a cool idea," and the mother agreed to try the plan.

For fathers, the sudden plunge into taking care of an adolescent son can be difficult. As his quest for independence conflicts with his wish to remain dependent, the boy can cause arguments. The father cited above said of his son in the new arrangement, "At first it was a daily struggle as he tried to exert power and I tried to control it while also trying to be a compassionate figure. Sometimes I get angry, tired, frustrated, but we have both grown and it has been worth it." He postponed some of his career goals and drastically restricted his social life.

The father who is willing and able to ask his son to live with him "may be better able to deal with the issues of adolescents, to set the boundaries and to keep them straight. What he can bring to their relationship is maleness, a concept of what it means to be an adult male and so a role model to whom the boy can relate in a very direct way," says Mary Dolan, assistant professor of social work at the Catholic University of America, who conducts family therapy.

When a change in home arrangements occasionally occurs, it almost always involves sons, rather than daughters, Ms. Brozan pointed out, because most girls already live with their mothers. However, she cites authorities on adolescence and divorce who disagree with the idea that a son should suddenly move in with his father on reaching adolescence. Dr. Ralph I. Lopez, clinical associate professor of pediatrics at New York Hospital, who specializes in the treatment of adolescents, says, "The argument that a boy needs a male environment in which to hone his male skills is fine, but to say that in order to achieve those skills he must live with the father is simply not true. It may create new problems. To uproot him may be a high price to pay for frequent access to the male parent."

Parents may also be ambivalent about the move. One mother said, "When Josh told me at the age of fourteen that he wanted to live full-time with his father, it was devastating. I felt very rejected." Under the joint-custody agreement, their son lived half the time with each parent. But as he reached mid-adolescence, he said, "I became tired of not having one home base."

The mother, looking back, summed up: "What helped was knowing it was a healthy move on his part. I knew that I'd have to go through letting go and feeling sad. Three years later, I realized it was not so bad. I had been the one to set all the limits in the past so there were lots of hassles over things like curfews. Now I am the weekend parent and have all the fun."

One woman sent her son to live with his father a thousand miles away, saying, "A son needs to claim his manhood, and that is hard to do in a family of women." The mother, Jane

Adams, wrote a book, *Good Intentions*, about her experience. She stated: "I believe that the very fact of a big strong male presence is a great comfort to teenagers. They feel strength from their fathers that, in spite of the women's movement, they don't feel from their mothers. And when a woman is strong, independent and liberated, in some cases that seems to rob her son of exactly what he needs at that time: a clear delineation between the sexes and a male role model."

SIBLINGS IN A "NEW" FAMILY

Many articles, even movies and TV films, focus on children whose parents remarry. Children have to adjust to a strange new father or mother, and this requires, on the part of both parent and children, much mutual understanding before the relationships can become fairly normal. The relationships can never duplicate the original one between the child and his or her own mother or father, but if both sides are willing to try to work things out, conflicts can be held to a minimum.

If both parents have children, it will not be easy for either to handle the ambivalent feelings of their own children toward the new parent, or to the children of the new spouse, who will be seen as additional rivals for the parent's love. But, as in the first marriage, honesty with the children is the best policy. Parents should allow the children to voice their feelings, informing them that feelings of ambivalence are to be expected and that it will take time for everyone to feel at home. The parents can, by their own example, show through love and trust of the new marital partner what they hope the children will express among themselves and to the stepparent.

In the new family, stepparents have to try to resolve their competitive feelings toward the natural parents. It is normal to wish to do them one better. Often, a stepparent feels jealous of the relationship between his or her stepchildren and the new spouse. Usually, this is an expression of the stepparent's insecurity in the new marriage and often indicates that the stepparent is worried that the second marriage will end as the first did. These issues require marital counseling and should be kept away from the children as much as possible.

In the newly created family, especially if the children are in their late teens, there may be temptation for sexual pairing to take place between the unrelated siblings. Not only is this natural because close living facilitates such relationships, but there is often the unconscious wish in two adolescents to duplicate the behavior of their parents, their role models.

In such a situation, the newly married parents can try to communicate to each other their anxiety, distress, and forbidden excitement in the sexual behavior of their child and stepchild. They may require some therapeutic aid in coming to grips with new and old feelings of self-doubt, competition, and troubled feelings.

With younger siblings, the danger is that they will start to express violent feelings against the members of the new family, using them as scapegoats for the anger and envy formerly expressed at their own siblings. Violent and angry feelings are inevitable. The siblings need to be accepted and their emotions tolerated by parents. But sanctions must be placed against acting on violent impulses.

One of the ways parents can help their children when two families are merged is by first acknowledging to the children, in advance of the marriage, that changes are always difficult and that resentments are inevitable, no matter what the changes are. Second, it is often helpful for the children to verbalize their fears and resentments. Third, before the families actually begin living with each other, it is often helpful for the families to have several get-togethers and to note, first privately then together, what some of the difficulties are. Sometimes, joint family conferences whereby all the members share their feelings, within appropriate limits placed by the adults, can calm the atmosphere. Finally, two families can become better adjusted to each other when the two adults who are getting married identify with each other, empathize with each other, and tolerate each other's limitations with love and equanimity.

OTHER ONE-PARENT HOMES FOR SIBLINGS

There are siblings who live with a mother or father who never married. Such siblings will have many conflicts to resolve since they will inevitably seek two parents and somehow will find, perhaps in fantasy, a replacement for the missing parent.

What makes these families somewhat different is that the parents have never felt the pleasures and the limitations and frustrations of living with a partner. For these parents to help their children, they need to consider some of their inhibitions and possible resentments toward the opposite sex. They also need to try their best to provide substitute parents for the children. Otherwise, the children may feel emotionally overburdened and unhappy with their lot in life.

11

THE ADOLESCENT SIBLING

THE AGONY OF ADOLESCENCE

To appreciate the problems of the adolescent sibling, it is helpful to review some highlights of adolescence, a most difficult phase of emotional development. Adolescence is a particularly sensitive, sometimes precarious time.

Literary portrayals of the perils of adolescence have been eloquent, starting with the Elizabethan era. *Romeo and Juliet* depicts the tragedy of adolescent adoration when families are mortal enemies and forbid romance to flower. Shakespeare's *Hamlet* shows a teenager responding to anxieties about his sexual identity. In more modern times Mark Twain wrote of the adolescent in 19th-century America in *The Adventures of Tom Sawyer* and *Adventures of Huckleberry Finn*. Most recently, J. D. Salinger in *Catcher in the Rye* poignantly depicts adolescent self-doubt and conflict.

Many young readers during the past few decades have identified with Holden Caulfield as they live through his swings from the height of elation to the depths of despair within a single hour. Parents describe teenagers as full of life one day, absolutely deflated the next. One minute they fight their parents' advice, then a moment later seek it desperately. In trying to establish their identity and autonomy, teenagers assert, in effect, "I rebel, therefore I am."

For centuries many adults, including those who studied child psychology, believed that sexuality started at puberty. It was quite common for parents to say nothing to their children about sex. When the child reached thirteen or fourteen years old he or she was given a book about the birds and the bees. One of Freud's great contributions was his recognition that sexuality begins at birth and that the infant at the breast is in many ways as sexual a being as the two-year-old preoccupied with urinating and defecating. The child of three or four who plays house, fantasizes about being married to the parent of the opposite sex, or plays doctor and patient is also expressing sexual interest.

Contemporary psychologists are re-examining what takes place between the ages of six and ten, called the "latency period," when sexual drives supposedly become dormant. But, since there is now more mingling between boys and girls in classrooms, on the dance floors, and on Little League baseball teams, it seems that the disappearance of sexuality during this period may have had more to do with the fears, denials, and impositions of parents and society than with any diminution of the child's sexual interest.

Adolescence is far from the start of sexuality. Rather, it recapitulates the sexual growth of the past twelve or thirteen years, as psychoanalyst Ernest Jones points out. The teenager feels intensely sexual, and at the same time relives past sexual feelings, experiences, and fantasies as they spring anew within.

The adolescent revives the oral period by dieting or indulging in peculiar food preferences, such as gorging on ice cream. The adolescent adds to this a new craving to use the mouth for passionate kissing. Then, reminiscent of the anal period, the teenager indulges in scatological language, tells and listens to dirty jokes, and frequently lives in unwashed, unpressed clothes as though they were a uniform.

The adolescent also reenacts the family romance of childhood fantasy. This now takes the form of falling in love with a schoolteacher, film hero, TV star, or rock-and-roll singer, all of whom substitute for the mother and father.

What makes adolescence a period of *Sturm und Drang* is the fact that the adolescent, as at no other time in life, is torn by two strong opposing pulls. On the one hand, the teenager wants to be a mature adult, now biologically capable of becoming a parent; yet, on the other hand, the teenager feels intense childish passions. He or she yearns to be a strong, independent adult, more powerful, more sexual, and more brilliant than the parents, but also wants to be a little baby, fed and indulged consistently.

Anna Freud has gone so far as to say that "a steady equilibrium during the adolescent process is abnormal." She points out that it is normal for an adolescent to behave, for a considerable time, in an inconsistent and unpredictable manner—to fight impulses and to accept them, to ward them off successfully and to be overcome by them, to love the parents and to hate them, to revolt against them and to depend on them, to be "deeply ashamed to acknowledge his mother before others and unexpectedly to desire heart to heart talks with her."

When a friend's youngest son was fifteen and making one of his frequent assessments of his father, first he told his father that he was too imposing and too concerned about his son. As the father sought to explore what he meant, the son complained, "You don't spend enough time with me." He was saying the father gave him too much attention on the one hand and too little on the other. The father couldn't win. When parents can accept the fact that the adolescent never wants them to be right for too long, they can preserve some of their sanity.

A sensitive mother of a fourteen-year-old girl complained, "My daughter is driving me crazy." One of many tormenting moments occurred when the daughter asked if she should wear the red satin or the blue organdy to a party. The mother advised, "I think the red dress looks better on you." Whereupon the daughter retorted, "Why do you have such poor taste?" This shows how difficult a teenager can be, how little thoughtfulness there is at times for the feelings of a parent.

Parents often become agonized by their adolescents because

they forget that, by definition, adolescents are the most ambivalent beings in the world. One day they speak like terrorists, the next like radical right-wingers. One day they want to feed the starving peoples of the world, the next they are so narcissistic they do not care about a sibling. Parents will feel more secure in living with adolescents if they accept the fact that instability, indecisiveness, inconsistency, and mood swings are par for the course.

SEXUALITY AND VIOLENCE

Just as the experiences of a young child help to develop the child's character, view of himself or herself, view of life, what happens during adolescence can influence the decades to come. One of the most obvious changes is that the adolescent feels, as never before, a sexual being. How parents, teachers and peers respond to this burgeoning sexuality will influence the child's self-image, self-esteem, and personal relationships.

If parents are threatened by what seems like a sudden sexual bent, the child may go to either extreme—promiscuity, in defiance of the parents, or celibacy, as though carrying out the parents' fear of sex to the point of denial. Or the child may swing between the two extremes.

An adolescent girl of fifteen said at her first therapy session that she intended to have nothing to do with boys; she wanted only a career and the idea of marriage was repulsive. By the next session, two days later, she revealed that she had fallen in love, was going steady, and planned to marry within a year. As therapy progressed, the extremity of her moods diminished. She neither went steady or completely resisted boys but dated a few and eventually lost the madly-in-love attitude.

A close-to-universal defense that adolescents show in coping with sexuality is what the psychoanalyst Dr. Franz Alexander called bribing the superego. The teenager is constantly trying to placate his or her conscience because the child strongly wishes to satisfy the sexual urges but feels they are evil. For instance, teenagers may reason, it's okay to pet above the waist but not below. Or, it's okay to neck on the second date but not the first. Or, it's okay to have sexual intercourse if you arrange to go steady. These compromises are an attempt to appease the conscience and ease guilt feelings about sexual desire.

Such compromises are not as predominant today as in the past because of the shift in teenage morality, which has led to promiscuous sex and unwanted pregnancies, as well as to temporary, unhappy marriages. This behavior has deeply upset parents who during their teenage years led a far more restricted sexual life than their adolescent children do. It is difficult for the parents to accept what they believe to be abhorrent behavior in their children.

When parents have trouble tolerating their adolescents' sexual preoccupation or acts, they must first ask whether their feelings are impeding their ability to help their teenagers. Promiscuity is not wise for teenagers—or those of any age—but scolding, lecturing and punishing adolescents will in no way stop their sexual activities. They have to be slowly helped to realize that promiscuity is born of despair and self-doubt and that it is these feelings parents and teenagers should face together.

Psychologists have likened the storms of adolescence to schizophrenia. As a matter of fact, the former medical term for schizophrenia, *dementia praecox*, is translated from the Greek as disease of adolescence. The extreme narcissism, the deep emotional instability, and the wild temper tantrums of adolescence all suggest a very disturbed young person. Some adolescents even act like a catatonic schizophrenic, withdrawn and silent. Celibacy is the choice of adolescent boys and girls so terrified of their strong sexual impulses that they wish to flee them by denying them. Denial is one of our strongest defenses against awareness of feelings that cause shame or pain.

Violent impulses may become so intense that adolescents commit suicide, either directly by turning a gun on themselves or hanging themselves, or indirectly by taking to drugs and alcohol. We live at a time when adolescent suicide is at its height and adolescent homicides and lesser crimes are widespread. On the one hand, some adolescents try to curb violent feelings in the ubiquitous use of drugs, but on the other indulge in violence as they steal money to pay for their addiction. There is a temporary easing of violent thoughts and wishes in the euphoria alcohol and drugs bring, an instant gratification of the wish to return to the peace of infancy in the sensations of the high alcohol and drugs offer.

When an adolescent's sexual and violent impulses cannot find an outlet in a nondestructive way, such as study, creativity, sports, or warm friendships, those impulses will find release in destructive ways. Parents should understand this need so they can encourage teenagers to enjoy constructive outlets, rather than seek destructive ones out of desperation and hopelessness.

THE ADOLESCENT AND YOUNGER SIBLINGS

Most adolescents have difficulty with their siblings, and most siblings of adolescents have trouble with them. Let us first look at the relationship the adolescent may establish with younger siblings. When we consider the adolescent, by definition, as an ambivalent, moody soul, the vacillations are bound to be felt not only by parents but by younger siblings as well. Some days, the adolescent will appear to be a generous, giving big brother or sister. The next day the adolescent will seem a monster telling the younger sibling to drop dead or get lost.

When an adolescent is very provocative to or rejecting of younger siblings, he or she is envying them because they seem to have fewer conflicts. The adolescent denigrates the young sibling as a stupid kid who doesn't know anything. One of the problems of the older adolescent in regard to younger siblings is that at times the adolescent wishes to be a younger sibling— free to be dependent, unperturbed by anxieties about the future, sexual desires, and murderous and suicidal fantasies. When the adolescent expresses envy that the younger one has it easier, this is not very different from the jealousy older people sometimes feel toward the younger generation.

Parents may find it difficult to acknowledge how envious and confused the adolescent feels toward a younger sibling because parents, along with other adults, often idealize the adolescent period and adolescents. Therapists have found that parents often consider the teenager their role model or ego ideal. Our fashions sometimes follow teenagers' dress and hairstyle, such as the recent punk hairdos for women and the beards and long hair for young men in the late 1960s and 1970s. Parents do not help their adolescents or themselves if they accept the adolescent as a role model, for often this is a way-out image, emotional miles from maturity.

It is difficult at times to be the younger brother or sister of a teenager. A friend recalls with some regret when his younger son, ten years old, wanted his older brother, thirteen, to be his mentor, companion and guide but was rejected on more than one occasion. The younger sibling sought his adolescent sibling as a parental substitute and felt depressed when rebuked. A sibling is apt to react with anger at rejection, and another sibling power struggle begins in the home.

But there are also many times when the adolescent will help the younger child, in spite of dating, homework, or getting ready for college. A sixteen-year-old girl always found time for her sister, ten years younger. The older sibling helped her younger one in her studies, took her shopping and to the movies, and encouraged her to grow up slowly, giving what was obviously maternal love and attention.

Often, it is helpful to the younger sibling to be told that the adolescent has troubles of his or her own and that the moody behavior has nothing to do with the younger sibling. And just as it is imperative for parents to empathize with the agony of the adolescent, it is equally important to help the younger sibling understand that there may be occasional rejection and abandonment by someone to whom the child has felt close over the years.

How this dilemma is resolved often has to do with the parent's own position in his or her own family. If the parent was the younger sibling with a teenage brother or sister, it is easy to overidentify with the younger sibling's plight and to be angry at the older sibling. But if the parent was an older sibling who resented the younger one, the parent may overidentify with the older sibling and turn the younger into a scapegoat.

Because the parent with both adolescent and younger children so often feels overwhelmed, this may account for the popularity of boarding schools, camps, colleges, and other institutions for adolescents. At least for a while, the house will seem more peaceful.

The parent of an adolescent with younger siblings would do well to recognize that times have changed and that the adolescent of the 1980s is very different from the adolescent of the parent's youth; to realize with some equanimity that the parent is no longer as young as he or she once was and that teenagers are enjoying more carefree times; to withstand constant attempts by the teenager to demean the parent's authority and status—it is particularly painful for parents to take even mild objections from someone to whom they have given so much over so many years; to realize that the younger siblings of the adolescent, just by virtue of being younger, have their own trials and torments.

WHEN THERE ARE TWO TEENAGE SIBLINGS

Two or more adolescent siblings frequently have a difficult time with each other. Because the adolescent vacillates in interests and attitudes he or she invariably presents problems to teenage siblings even though they experience the same see-saw of emotions. One may be up when the other is down. Each projects his or her own dire thoughts on the other and blames the other for what goes wrong. They may avoid each other for periods of time, possibly threatened by each other's sexuality, especially if one is a boy and one a girl.

Since the adolescent has an unstable body image and self-image, and is always changing his or her mind about everything—politics, religion, vocational choice, or love object— when there are two adolescents in a family, parents often are the recipients of double-barreled attacks. Sometimes, each teenager describes a different fault of the parents, while on other occasions siblings present a united front.

An adolescent brother and sister may be trying to cope with sexual attraction to each other. This is hard enough to deal with in the formative years, but in adolescence the intensity of their feelings may prove quite painful. On the one hand they feel strong sexual desires, and on the other they must curb their sexual wishes because of the incest taboo. Thus, they frequently battle to ward off sexual attraction. If parents can say soothingly, you two may be afraid to admit that you like each other, teenagers are more likely to cooperate rather than wage an endless war.

Some adolescents behave promiscuously as they try to ward off sexual fantasies toward a sibling. A man married five times consulted a therapist because he was afraid his fifth marriage was breaking up and he wanted to save it, if he could. He confessed that in each marriage he fell in love, proposed, enjoyed a prolonged honeymoon, and then found himself in a tempestuous struggle with the woman—that was the theme of all his failed marriages. He said, "I'm beginning to realize that I, not the woman, am the source of my failure."

In one session, he revealed that all five of the wives were the oldest sister in their families. He also reported that during his adolescence he was possessed by ardent sexual feelings and fantasies about his oldest sister. As therapy progressed, he became aware that he had substituted his wives for his beloved sister. He had turned his wives into older sisters, a role they were all too willing to assume, since they were the oldest sisters in their families. He then had to punish himself for breaking the incest taboo by wrecking the marriage. He was finally able to see his fifth wife in her own right and to break the pattern of feeling angry at her, then guilty, and then rejecting her as a sibling temptress.

Teenage brothers and sisters can become enemies because they feel ashamed of their warm, loving feelings. Here again, parents can be helpful to feuding teenagers by assuring them that enmity is a way of denying their closeness, which need not end in sexual acting out. When teenagers become more accepting of their sexual fantasies they can enjoy friendship and love, with its mutual respect, trust, caring, and protectiveness.

Teenage siblings are also ambivalent as to how much to depend on each other. A teenager may wish to use a teenage sibling as a confidante, with whom to discuss dates, schoolwork, and plans for the future. But the teenager may also be afraid of a dependency on the sibling similar to the one he or she feels on the parents. So one teenager repudiates the other. Or, one teenager will ask advice from another then angrily refuse to take it as a power struggle emerges. The teenager who asks a sibling for help reasons, I want to feel close to my sibling, his or her advice is helpful, but if I accept it I become a little child asking my parents and I have to show my sibling he or she doesn't have that much control over me.

Parents can encourage teenagers to consult each other, pointing out that they will not become a dependent infant by taking advice from a sibling. Even if a teenager does not take an older sibling's advice, he or she will enjoy the freedom to consult the sibling.

Teenage siblings compete in many areas. Hungry in countless ways, they wish to be the greatest intellectual, the most talented athlete, the best dancer, the closest friend, and the most skillful lover. Because they are unsure of who they are, they are jealous of a sibling's slightest moment in the limelight. Sometimes they viciously attack a successful younger sibling and repudiate his or her achievements because of an envy they cannot tolerate.

Sometimes an older sibling will give up, feeling it is useless to compete with a younger one, as will younger siblings who fear the wrath of the older one. A fifteen-year-old girl in therapy was an "A" student yet felt deeply depressed. She said her older brother constantly scoffed at her high marks and popularity in school. She was afraid to show her anger at his contempt, and instead turned the anger against herself. She admitted she was even willing to fail in her classes if her brother would stop criticizing her and admire her as he formerly did. The therapist helped her understand that her brother was jealous of her, and when she accepted this she was able to continue her excellent record in school and to keep up with her many friendships. Also, when she became more self-assured, her brother stopped his harassment, realizing he no longer had such a submissive target for his hostility. Like all teenagers, she also felt guilty about her competitive wishes, wanting to better her brother's record but not daring to face her own competitiveness.

A therapist once worked with an eighteen-year-old girl who

made therapeutic progress but did not completely give up her depression. One day, she admitted she felt guilty about being more successful in school than her brother, a year younger. This eighteen-year-old could not tolerate her competitive fantasies. Success, for many of us, is taboo because in the unconscious we have the fantasy we are killing off siblings or other competitors.

Some parents become so upset by the competition among their teenage siblings that, in their attempts to reduce it, they emphasize the similarities between the two children. This only makes the siblings more furious because they do not want to be similar. When parents feel secure in the knowledge that any two teenage siblings will possess unique strengths and unique assets, and tell them so, some of the competition will be reduced.

One father was uncomfortable when he observed that his younger son seemed more athletic than his older son, who prided himself on being quite an athlete. The father inadvertently reassured the older boy as to his athletic prowess, but this son sensed that his father protested too much and felt his father's reassurance was actually a disguised putdown. The father then accepted the fact that his younger son was the better athlete, and this helped both sons to pursue their independent goals with more pleasure and security. The older son devoted more time and energy to his major interest, international relations, and the younger became a three-letter man in college. Parents can be more helpful to teenagers when they deal not with the competitive spirit but with the individuals and their unique interests and inclinations.

Teenagers often compete over clothes and peers. The competition can become intense if the teenagers do not feel secure about their sexuality. One mother of two teenage girls became upset because her daughters fought over dress styles, boys, and their different ideas about love. The intensity of their battles was reduced when the mother talked to them about their right to disagree peaceably, and about sex in general. As she helped her daughters feel less competitive and less guilty about sexual feelings, their fights diminished.

Sometimes two teenagers choose to fall in love with the same person. When this happens, they may well be actually feuding over their parents' affections. The issue to be faced here is their competitive attraction to their parent, so that each sibling will then find his or her own special friend, rather than wishing to share the same one.

THE TEENAGER WITH AN OLDER SIBLING

When an adolescent has a sibling in his or her twenties, the latter, who has just passed through teenage turmoil, may find the younger sibling's impulsivity, intensity, and burgeoning sexuality difficult to bear. The older sibling may, in essence, forsake the younger sibling, leaving the teenager to his or her own errors.

But, sometimes the older sibling will lend a helping hand, and then the teenager can derive much solace from this relationship. The older sibling is not a parent, and thus the threat to the teenager of increased dependency is not as acute. The teenager is more willing to consider the advice of an older sibling. Parents should welcome this mentorship, not feel threatened in any way if a fifteen-year-old seems to feel closer to an older brother or sister than to them. Many teenagers seek a leader in their lives younger than their parents, and this is why teachers, athletic instructors, and community leaders are often so popular among adolescents.

It is no easy matter for parents, as they feel the waning of their power over the adolescent, to watch the teenager confiding in an older sibling, friends, and teachers. But parents should accept their particular solace—their victory in helping the teenager to feel free to talk over life's problems with people he or she trusts. In choosing confidantes other than the parents, the teenager is asserting independence, an independence the teenager will need as he or she goes out into the world. Parents should consider this new ability an achievement on their part.

THE ADOLESCENT SET FREE

All through a child's life, parents should be aware of the

need to help the child build a sturdy sense of independence so that by the time the child leaves home for good, he or she feels confident enough to make it on his or her own. This requires parents who gradually give a child a sense of trust in himself or herself and who have the faith and strength to go it alone.

There is a world of difference between parents exercising authoritarian control over a child and using protectiveness and guidance. Control is an angry, demanding feeling that implies, you must do exactly as I say, whereas protectiveness and guidance implies, let me help you avoid realistic dangers, become more independent and gain a sense of your self-worth. Control leads to rebellion and destructiveness of the self and/or of others, whereas protection and guidance lead to a child's easy maturing.

Parents, as they lose their influence over teenagers, should be careful to avoid power struggles with the children. Adolescents do grow up, become more stable, and less ambivalent. Parents also have to realize that they may feel somewhat jealous of those the teenagers now seek out for comfort, love, and direction. Many parents would also like to be teenagers again, envious of the spontaneity, exuberance, and freedom of the adolescent.

Some parents, especially those who experienced a very inhibited adolescence themselves, live vicariously through their teenagers, unwittingly pushing them into early sexual liaisons, social activities, and academic achievement. Parents would do well to examine their feelings to see whether they feel jealous of their adolescents or are encouraging them to carry out their own secret desires, or both. Things are seldom clear cut where emotions are concerned, but rather a combination of many different feelings and fantasies.

There are parents who have little trouble setting their adolescents free. These parents wish to relax from the long years of tumult, ambivalence, anxiety, provocativeness, and rebellion in the home. Bringing up an adolescent in the 1980s is no easy time for a parent because standards of behavior have so drastically changed. But the emotional storms of adolescence do diminish, much as a high fever eventually wanes. The later years are likely to be happier for both parents and adolescents, especially if the parents have encouraged the child from the start to develop a spirit of independence and the ability to choose wisely when making an important decision. Such emotional education will also help the adolescent to develop a far more tranquil and pleasurable relationship with a member of the opposite sex and with his or her own children.

We could say that civilization achieves new heights in emotional upbringing when parents accord adolescents the right to make their own mistakes and learn from them, rather than always being controlled by adults. Learning by rote is not as meaningful as learning through our own mistakes. The former is imposed on us, the latter we achieve from within, emotionally as well as intellectually. It is the emotional dimension that gives depth to learning.

Parents also should not be afraid to tell an adolescent or a younger child, I was wrong, I am sorry. It is difficult for a parent to admit to a child that he or she made a mistake, but it is extremely important to the child to hear a parent say this, because then the child does not have to be perfect. Nor does the child become disillusioned and lose self-esteem when he or she makes an error.

Setting free adolescents, painful though this may be for parents, will bring rewards to both parents and children. Parents do well to understand the value of letting go. Their child will be forever grateful, and the parents can take pride in a difficult but highly rewarding task.

12

WHEN IS
THERAPY INDICATED?

TIME TO SEEK A THERAPIST

We have stressed the similarity between adults and children who are in therapy and those who are not in therapy because we recognize that many parents, despite their sophistication, may still find it difficult to accept counseling for themselves or for their children. There are times, however, when parents should consider getting professional help for their children and themselves.

Let us take five examples.

1. When the child's problems are intense and frequent, this is usually an indication that therapy is needed. For example, if a child's sibling rivalry shows itself with frequent temper tantrums, such as three or four times a week, this suggests that the child feels emotionally overwhelmed and needs a neutral place and a person who is less involved than the parents in

order to deal with his or her feelings.

Or if a child's withdrawal, the opposite of a temper tantrum, is intense and frequent, this too is an indication for therapy. Certain children are so frightened of their anger toward siblings and parents that they inhibit their feelings and keep themselves from expressing any sign of anger. When a child withdraws from conversation, and habitually finds it difficult to be involved in any way with the mother and father, the siblings, or with other adults or children, the child is probably experiencing emotional pain too intense for a parent to handle alone.

2. When power struggles between the child and parents are continuous, with the child constantly provoking and disobeying the parent and the parent constantly feeling exasperated and angry, this is another indication that therapy is needed. Usually, when power struggles are strong between parents and a child, the child has some unconscious wish to defeat the parent's attempts to help; this is when a professional, less involved with the child on a day-to-day basis, might well be consulted.

Very often, a child is relieved when a parent finally says, We seem to be fighting a lot and I know it is hard for you to talk over your anger at your sister or brother with someone else. The child will feel less guilty for the provocative behavior and more respectful of the parent who now appears less omnipotent by admitting he can't do everything himself. The parent's statement also reflects concern and care for the child, who welcomes the parent's and therapist's special attention.

3. Another indication that therapy might be called for occurs when, despite all the parents' efforts to modify their attitudes and their behavior with a child, the child's problems persist. For example, if a parent finds that he or she becomes firmer and more consistent yet the child's conflict remains unchanged, therapy is indicated. Or, if the parent encourages more communication between himself or herself and the child, or between the child and a sibling, and the child withdraws or indulges in temper tantrums or the rivalry continues unabated, therapy is needed.

Many parents feel that if a child remains unresponsive to a new approach that there is something wrong with the parents, so they try even harder. In fact, certain maladaptive problems of children, such as provocative and withdrawn behavior, become habitual, and sometimes even the most caring parents cannot alter the child's need to behave this way. Just as it is not due to poor parenting when a child needs relief of severe flu by a doctor or pain from a toothache by a dentist, it is not indicative of poor parenting when a severe emotional conflict cannot be alleviated by a parent.

If the various suggestions we have made throughout this book have been tried by parents several times without much success, it suggests that the problem can be resolved only by professional help.

4. Another indication that therapy is needed occurs when parents receive reports from school, the community center, Boy Scout or Girl Scout leaders, or church officials that the child appears either very unhappy or finds it difficult to relate to other children. Certain children find it much easier to reveal their conflicts in school or some other place outside the home. This is why many parents are astonished when they hear from an outsider that their child is showing a problem. The statement, my child never acts this way at home, often is true, but many children feel less threatened when they show sibling rivalry in school rather than at home. They prefer that a teacher admonish them than that a parent do so, since the latter's love is more important to them. They prefer to risk the disapproval of a teacher.

While one or two statements about a child from a teacher or other adult are not sufficient to warrant therapy, because a child seems reasonably well-behaved at home does not necessarily mean that all is well. If there are several reports by a number of adults with common themes relating to excessive provocativeness or intense rivalry on the part of a child, the parents might wish to consult a professional.

5. The final indication for therapy is when children report their unhappiness to the parent, either directly or indirectly. When a child talks repeatedly about feeling sad or angry and the parent's reassuring remarks do not have much impact in alleviating the child's distress, this suggests that the child is asking for professional help.

In this age, when so many children receive help in child-guidance clinics, family agencies, and private therapy, it should not shock a parent to hear from a child: My friend has a therapist, why can't I have one? A four-year-old referred to a therapist as the appointment man and the child's friend said in envy, "I want an appointment man too." Child patients bring friends to their appointments who want the chance to be listened to or to take part in play therapy. Adults sometimes underestimate how much pleasure a child derives from being given the opportunity to talk to, and to be listened to, by a sympathetic adult. Many children have ways of making their desire for therapy known to parents, and this desire should be respected.

We are not suggesting that because a child is jealous of a friend who has a therapist that the parents should rush out to get a therapist, only that the parent should carefully listen to what a child wants from a therapist and why the child wants it. If a parent doubts the need for treatment, one or two consultations with a child therapist might be helpful in making a decision.

PREPARING YOURSELF AND YOUR CHILD FOR THERAPY

Many parents believe that therapy is a long drawn-out procedure lasting many years and costing large sums of money. In most cases, therapy for a child can be successful within the space of several months or, at most, a year or two. Children are very fluid and flexible, and they generally respond much better to therapy than adults. Children are frequently less reluctant than adults to accept the authority of a therapist. The idea of talking about their feelings and having their feelings addressed is so reassuring for most children that often an interpretation from a therapist can resolve a conflict very quickly.

A three-year-old boy was constantly obsessed with dirt on the floor and, despite his loving parents' reassurance, his fear and concern persisted. The therapist realized that this child was feeling very worried about not becoming fully toilet-trained. As a result, the boy feared that he might act on his forbidden wishes to urinate or defecate on the floor and be punished for it, or lose his parents' respect. By watching the dirt on the floor carefully, he was really watching himself carefully, making sure that he would control himself and not make a mess on the floor.

When the therapist suggested to him that, like all boys and girls at the age of three, he would occasionally wish to urinate or dirty on the floor but feared his mother or father would be angry, he laughed and felt reassured that he was not alone in the world with such a fear or wish. When the therapist explained the boy's dilemma to the parents and suggested they tell their son it was quite possible he might have accidents and they would understand, not punish, the boy's fear disappeared. He no longer watched the dirt on the floor. The entire therapy consisted of three sessions with the boy and two sessions with his parents.

When children are four or younger, consultation with the parents alone, without any therapy for the child, can be helpful. But when the child is five and older, consultation with the parents alone cannot always eradicate the difficulties. However, it is frequently helpful for parents to work alone with the therapist first, to understand themselves and their children better, and see if this work by itself may diminish the child's problem.

Before introducing the idea of therapeutic help to a child, the parent, as with anything else in the child's life, has to be comfortable with the notion. If a parent feels that the child's being in therapy is an indictment that he or she is a bad parent, he or she may unconsciously try to sabotage the therapy. Also, if the parent feels that therapy for the child is indicative of craziness in either the child or the parent, the parent will find it difficult to introduce the idea of therapy to the child. Almost always, when a child is reluctant to take part in therapy, it is because one or both parents are reluctant. Consequently, whenever a parent suggests therapy to his child and the child consistently balks at the idea, the parent should ask: What about therapy for my child do *I* oppose?

This is not an easy question. It takes courage and sometimes hard work to face one's fears and prejudices. But any time a child opposes something a parent wants the child to do, it is always helpful, whether it be therapy, schoolwork, cleaning up a room, or stopping sibling fights, for the parent to ask: What is my own reluctance in this matter?

Once a parent has overcome his or her own fear and resistance to the idea of therapeutic help, the parent can then prepare the child to accept it. As with most things, the simpler and shorter, the better. For example, a parent can say to a child: We've tried our best to help you and you've tried your best to get along better with your sibling, but you're still unhappy. We would like you to see someone who can help you feel better about yourself so you can get along better with your sibling.

Usually children want to know what will happen with the therapist. Here a parent can tell the child that he or she will meet once or twice a week with the therapist to talk about whatever bothers the child—what his brother or sister does to annoy the child, what uncomfortable feelings he or she has around the house, what makes the child unhappy. If the child is under twelve, the chances are he or she will be seen in play therapy, and here the parents can explain that most children show what troubles them by drawing pictures, telling stories, playing games like checkers or chess, or playing house or doctor.

This sort of dialogue helps most children feel comfortable enough to meet the therapist for the first time and, as we have said, if the child senses that the parent feels comfortable with the therapist, usually the child will feel that way too. We cannot emphasize enough how important it is for the successful outcome of therapy that the parent feel warmly and positively toward the child's therapist. Therefore, it is imperative that the parent meet the therapist before the child does and make sure that the therapist is someone whom the parent trusts. If the parent does not feel comfortable with the child's therapist, the child will not either.

As therapy progresses, many parents become very curious as to what goes on. It is best for parents not to pry but to let the child tell them what he or she wishes them to know. This may be difficult for parents as they watch the child develop a relationship outside the home, perhaps for the first time. Parents may feel jealous or rivalrous, and a certain amount of these feelings are inevitable. Parents should not berate themselves for feeling competitive when the child confides in another adult. The child will probably feel more warmly and more accepting of the parents if they do not try to delve into what goes on in therapy.

Usually, parents also need to be seen for some counseling while their child is in therapy. We have found that whether the parents see a child therapist or some other therapist, this only enhances a positive outcome.

Both parents are deemed important when a child is in therapy, as the parents are involved in counseling to reinforce the child's experiences and to understand their own roles in the persistence of the child's problems.

An adolescent is often more difficult to prepare for treatment than a younger child, since the adolescent has very mixed feelings toward all adults. Consequently, anything a parent suggests will be questioned. Even if a parent advises the therapy, it is best, if the adolescent refuses to accept the idea, that the parents respect the child's resistance and not get into a power struggle. If the teenager senses the parents' good intentions and the parents do not argue about the therapy, the teenager may very well agree to the idea, perhaps not at once but weeks or months later.

Many therapists who work with children point out that a child who has had several months or a year or two of psychotherapy probably functions and feels better than most other children. This is probably also true for those adults who have had a chance to talk about their conflicts. Therapy, whether for an adult or a child, is a form of education. To educate oneself about oneself can be an enriching and enhancing experience.

13

RAISING A
HAPPY SIBLING

IS HAPPINESS POSSIBLE?

In considering the characteristics of a happy sibling, we should examine first what makes a child happy. We all wish to live happily ever after, yet happiness seems ephemeral and elusive. To be happy is the highest goal of life—consciously speaking. Unconsciously, however, other goals clash with our desire to be happy, goals such as greed, lust, jealousy, and revenge. From a psychoanalytic point of view, constant and consistent happiness is all but impossible, even with the best parents providing the best possible childhood for their offspring. Why is constant happiness virtually impossible?

Growing up carries with it the many frustrations necessary to become civilized. Society, and parents, demand that children act in a civilized way. Infants have to cope with the times that parents are not immediately available. The idea that an infant's first months on earth are blissfully happy is erroneous. Infants cry as they express their pain and frustration, not only when parents are absent, but when a diaper is full, or the breast or bottle is not available at once.

Every infant also goes through the first major frustration— weaning. The child learns sooner or later that he or she cannot always have a breast or bottle when desired, and this causes the child to feel unhappy and cry out in pain and anguish. But no sooner does the child accept the reality that permanent attachment to a breast is no longer part of life than another frustration occurs—toilet-training. No child welcomes the idea of being told to urinate or defecate in a pot; he or she feels frustration and inevitable anger at having to control these bodily urges. This is why we hear the two-year old saying, day in and day out, No! No! and why parents and professionals refer to this stage of development as the terrible twos. During the second year of life, children have to accept certain limitations that induce anger and unhappiness.

As soon as the child acquires mastery over sphincter control, learning to handle another segment of reality with some confidence, the child is introduced to still other frustrations. He or she is not allowed to enter the parental bedroom at night. The child feels strong competition with the parent of the same sex, fantasizing a romantic liaison with the parent of the opposite sex. These frustrated sexual wishes also prove a source of unhappiness.

The child becomes subject to many rules, and is furious that he or she cannot turn the parents and siblings into pawns who serve the child. The original nature of infancy holds a selfish tinge which the child has to learn to turn into a generous frame of mind in order to get along with others, including siblings.

As children learn to accept the fact that they cannot rule the house, they come up against other major frustrations. They must leave the familiarity of home and go to school, share the affection of a teacher, achieve high grades, get along with peers. As they become involved in clubs, the Girl Scouts and Boy Scouts, athletic teams, they realize they have to cooperate in a group, that they cannot always be center stage.

Many of the conflicts we have mentioned in discussing sibling rivalry occur in the early years of school, when the child realizes he or she cannot be the recipient of constant love and adoration—some classmates may even hate the child, out of their own conflicts or because the child has been unable to give up the sense of omnipotence. And the era of adolescence, though idealized and glorified, is far from a happy time. Rather, it is a time of turbulence, distress, and confusion about the developing self—though the happier earlier childhood has been, the less agonizing adolescence will be.

Given all these pitfalls to be negotiated in growing up, no child can be consistently happy. No child lives without frustrations or receives what the psychological epicurean demands. The nearest we can come to a happy childhood is to accept with good grace the many frustrations and feelings of anger, depression, envy, and greed they bring so that we learn to act in a civilized fashion.

THE MATURE CHILD

The quiet acceptance of a certain amount of frustration leads a child to maturity. Maturity can be achieved on a relatively permanent basis. A mature child, or for that matter a mature adult, accepts reality, with its frustrations, limitations, and, at times, profound disappointments, with equanimity—rather than fighting it with fury.

The mature child enjoys life to a certain extent and also accepts, without too much protest, that life cannot be perfect. The mature child, most of the time, has a peaceful attitude, is reflective and slow to anger, and rarely sinks into depression. The mature child puts his or her energy into learning about the world, living in harmony with siblings, offering to help them, and asking for help when needed.

For a child to be mature, and therefore happy much of the time, he or she needs the type of parenting we have described throughout this book. Such parenting requires a mother and father who basically like, respect, and trust each other. In this day and age, unfortunately, many children lack one parent because of the high rate of separation and divorce. And even when together, parents may engage in a competitive power struggle, unable to tame their primitive fantasies or accept their limitations. When a child's home holds the animosity of parents who fight with each other over who is right or who is in control, the child will be gripped by self-doubt, confusion, anger, and depression.

In raising a mature child, Reuben Fine's notion of the analytic ideal is a helpful concept. Fine points out that, while this ideal is rarely fully reached, it can be achieved in various degrees if children and adults experience primarily love rather than hate; enjoy realistic pleasures and accept realistic frustrations; have a sense of identity; possess a role in the family; accept sexual wishes without guilt; acknowledge a wide range of emotions; are able to communicate with freedom; and have an absence of neurotic symptoms such as phobias, compulsions, or deep depression.

To raise a child who comes close to the analytic ideal, parents should feel fairly consistent love and limited hatred, not only toward the child but also toward each other. They should enjoy ministering to an infant and welcome caring for a child without feeling exploited or deprived of their own pleasure. They should wean the child easily, accepting the child's wish to resist without feeling devastated or that they must punish him or her for not obeying immediately.

A mature parent has the freedom to say no in a firm, understanding manner during the stage of the terrible twos. When restrictions and limitations are placed on the child gradually but firmly by two cooperative parents, the child feels a sense of security, a growing identity, and a relative absence of anxiety. The mature child is able to witness parents who are comfortable kissing and hugging each other and can talk without embarrassment about sexuality with the child.

A child matures and starts to derive pleasure from life when the child knows that the parents have a relationship apart from the child, enjoying pleasures and privileges that do not involve the child. A mature child recognizes that parents are each other's exclusive bed partner and that their privacy must not be invaded. If the parent draws the child too much into the parent's emotional, sexual, or aggressive life, the child will feel a responsibility impossible to fulfill. The child will be haunted by the feeling of failure, the belief he or she will never be able to meet the parents' expectations.

A mature child's parents encourage the child to separate emotionally from the family, to enjoy school and to find friends. Parents are not threatened by other adults in the child's life who may wish to be close to the child, such as grandparents, aunts and uncles, teachers, or peers. If a child is helped to mature, adolescence will be less of a torment.

It is not easy to be a wise parent. A parent can only do his or her best, remembering his or her own parents' omissions and derelictions and forgiving them. It takes bravery to be an understanding parent and to be strong enough and willing enough to tackle his or her own conflicts of love and hate. Perhaps the most useful message we can give a parent who wants to raise relatively mature and happy siblings is try to know thyself as well as possible. If a parent is excessively dependent and has conflicts about sexuality, angry feelings, and a sense of identity, the parent will find it difficult to help the children because they possess the same conflicts.

THE MATURE SIBLING

Just as it requires two happy persons to have a happy marriage, it requires two happy children to have a happy sibling relationship. A mature sibling accepts that each sibling is entitled to as much love and attention as the other sibling gets. In fact, a mature sibling can tolerate a brother or sister receiving more attention at certain times, including a birthday or on attaining a special achievement.

The mature sibling cooperates with other siblings because he or she has seen the parents cooperate and experiences them as true allies. The mature sibling transmits this attitude to other siblings and gives them a respect due every member of the family.

How well a sibling copes with the competition and frustration entailed in being a sibling depends in large part on how the parents act in the face of competition, crisis, and frustration. By their attitudes and behavior, parents show their children how to deal with life's dilemmas. All children, no matter who their parents, identify with and imitate both the mother and father. If a child consistently observes parents arguing, fighting, and competing this is seen as an appropriate, normal way of conducting a relationship. When a father or mother are constantly petulant, irritable, and unsmiling, the child will imitate the parents.

A mature sibling, one who is reasonably happy throughout childhood into adulthood, usually has two mature parents who are reasonably happy with themselves and with their children. Happiness is contagious within a household. If the mother and father are compatible, trusting, and respectful of each other, they will not have to worry about their children. If concern, rather than confusion, permeates a home, siblings will reflect this in their thoughtful acts toward each other.

A happy child is the greatest reward a parent can receive. Somehow the knowledge that a parent has raised a contented, creative, companionable child brings the parent a feeling of having achieved the most important goal in life. A happy, mature child is a gift to the parent, a gift the parent has earned through bestowing on the child the parent's own gifts—love, understanding and the feeling that the child is respected, honored, and valued as a precious object in the parent's life.

When a parent gives faith and trust to the child, the parent receives the most cherished gift in life. Not money, not fame, not praise, but the knowledge that hard work and the efforts to understand and help the child mature rather than cause pain and emotional injury, has resulted in the real treasure we all seek—the knowledge that we will live on after death—as our children continue the chain of happiness that hopefully will grow from generation to generation.

The happier our children, the happier their children and the greater the chance of a happier world. Only the child whose parents have shown thoughtfulness, respect, and love is able, as an adult, to show such feelings to strangers, to people who may be different in color, faith, the rules they live by, or the government they pledge allegiance to.

For adults to be able to consider peace throughout the world means that, as children, they knew a certain peace in their homes, a peace that far outweighed the frictions that arose as part of daily living and adjusting to society's demands. The siblings who have been able to live with each other in comparative friendship and who care what happens to each other as they grow up are the ones who will care about forwarding the progress of world peace. Sir Thomas Browne wrote in his *Religio Medici*, in 1642, "*Charity begins at home,* is the voice of the world; yet is every man his greatest enemy, and, as it were, his own executioner." Love begins at home, and if it is present to a greater rather than lesser degree, man need not be his own executioner or his children's, but his own and their savior.

INDEX

TACKLE LIFE'S PROBLEMS

With Help From St. Martin's Press!